Nurturing a healthy mind

Michael C Nagel PhD is an Associate Professor in the School of Science and Education at the University of the Sunshine Coast, where he teaches and researches in the areas of human development, educational psychology, behaviour and learning. Dr Nagel has written a number of books and articles related to neurological development in children and has delivered over 200 workshops and seminars for parents and teachers nationally and internationally. He is also a member of the prestigious International Neuropsychological Society and a feature writer for the *Child* series of magazines, which offers parenting advice to more than one million Australian readers.

doing what matters most for your child's developing brain

Nurturing a healthy mind

Michael C Nagel PhD

First published 2012

Exisle Publishing Pty Ltd
'Moonrising', Narone Creek Road, Wollombi, NSW 2325, Australia
P.O. Box 60–490, Titirangi, Auckland 0642, New Zealand
www.exislepublishing.com

National Library of Australia Cataloguing-in-Publication Data:

Nagel, Michael C.

Nurturing a healthy mind : doing what matters most for your child's
developing brain / Michael C. Nagel.

ISBN 9781921966026 (pbk.)

Includes bibliographical references and index.

Brain—Growth.
Pediatric neuropsychology.
Cognitive neuroscience.
Child psychology.
Child rearing.
Parent and child.

155.413

Designed by Tracey Gibbs
Illustrations by Rebecca Mills
Typeset in Adobe Caslon Pro
Printed in Singapore by KHL Printing Co Pte Ltd

This book uses paper sourced under ISO 14001 guidelines from
well-managed forests and other controlled sources.

10 9 8 7 6 5 4 3 2 1

This book is dedicated to Emily. What I have learned about the developing brain is nothing compared to what Emily has taught me about being a loving and compassionate parent.

Contents

Introduction

What shall we do next?

All organisms with complex nervous systems are faced with the moment-by-moment question that is posed by life: What shall I do next?

— Sue Savage-Rumbaugh, primatologist, and Roger Lewin, anthropologist

I remember the day we took our first child, Madeline, home from the hospital. We had read plenty of parenting articles and received more advice from family, friends and colleagues than we were capable of remembering. To be honest, much of it we chose to forget. We had also waded through a sea of books on parenting, each with its own take on child rearing and how not to commit the misguided sins of days gone by. Yet, as I opened the door to the car, strapped Maddie into her government-approved baby safety capsule and checked her harness with the zeal of someone with obsessive-compulsive disorder, the question above kept reverberating in my mind ... what shall we do next? We had a new life in our hands; a beautiful daughter who was beginning to experience her first days out of the maternity ward along a protracted journey to independence.

Like all of those who will read this book, I have experienced many new things in my own life and, indeed, life is full of beginnings. However, nothing I had ever done prepared me for the overwhelming reality of raising another human being. The vast majority of my experiences with children were during my days as a schoolteacher and coach, and while this might have given me some insights into Maddie's future educational endeavours, I felt uneasy about my adequacy in having to deal with the tiny and vulnerable being sleeping in the back seat. I am assuming this sounds familiar to you and you may, at this very moment, be feeling something similar. Well, I have some good news! Take heart! You're not the first to have these doubts and you won't be the last, but at least you have an opportunity to know so much more about child development than I did over a decade ago and so much more than previous generations.

Interestingly, the reason why we know so much more today than our grandparents can be traced back to 17 July 1990. The 1990s were an amazing decade of change. Germany became a unified nation, Yugoslavia and the Soviet Union fell apart, Princess Diana and Prince Charles called it quits, the 'World Wide Web' became available to the masses, *Jurassic Park* was a hit movie and on 17 July 1990 President George Bush (senior) signed Presidential Proclamation 6158 dedicating the 1990s as the 'Decade of the Brain', thus making brain research a matter of important public policy (presidential proclamations are important initiatives of the US Congress signifying an emphasis on funding into areas of research deemed of major importance). Much of the initial research originating from this proclamation was designed to provide the public with a greater understanding of mental health issues, degenerative brain disorders and the effects of drugs on the brain; however, the signing of the document acted as a worldwide catalyst for research across a number of fields regarding the brain. Now, at the beginning of the twenty-first century, parents and teachers are seeing the benefits of that work, whereby child rearing and education are being shaped by new understandings of the human brain.

The human brain has been described as the most 'unimaginable thing imaginable' and we still know very little about it compared to what we would like to know. However, we do know that the interactions between our genetic makeup, early experiences and environmental influences shape the architecture of the developing brain and, as such, our understanding of the importance of the early years of life have, thankfully, received much greater attention and scrutiny. We are witnessing a tsunami of research, in conjunction with well-informed individuals, looking to ensure that all children receive the attention they need in their earliest days of life. Parents and early caregivers, therefore, have a great opportunity to tap into the research and provide the best environment possible for healthy child development. That is what this book is about.

The research that has stemmed from Proclamation 6158 has been used here to unlock many important questions and insights related to conception, birth and the early years of life, in particular, the significant life moments that provide us with an informed perspective towards ensuring our children have the best possible chance of healthy development. Specifically, insights into how the brain develops and matures into something entirely unimaginable offer us greater opportunities to make better decisions as parents and educators when we ask ourselves what we should do next.

It probably goes without saying that the vast majority of parents want to do what is best for their children. Often, however, doing what is best may not always happen early enough. For example, if parents knew that about seventeen days after conception the brain starts to take shape and that the consumption of alcohol during the early stages of pregnancy could have long-term consequences on neural development, how many mothers might reconsider when to stop drinking? In terms of healthy foetal development, perhaps knowing that waiting until a test confirms pregnancy might be too late would force some parents to reconsider their lifestyle choices. Perhaps this knowledge would persuade prospective parents that when the decision to start trying to have children is made then a decision to stop drinking might also need to be made. You see, our understanding of the intricacies of the brain has changed and with that must come changes to our understanding of doing what is best for our children.

Since President Bush's proclamation was made we have learned a great deal about the brain. Indeed, 95 per cent of the neuroscientists who ever lived are alive today and brain research continues to grow exponentially.

New research has provided us with opportunities to debunk old ideas about the brain and child development and to move forward in our understanding of that gelatinous mass between our ears. For example, neurobiological research tells us that the longer we wait to assist children who are at the greatest risk of poverty, neglect or abuse, the more difficult it becomes to help those children in the future grow into productive and healthy adults. In other words, we have learned that the experiences that fill a child's first days, months and years have a profound and decisive impact on the overall development of their brain which, in turn, will impact on the nature and extent of their adult capabilities. This book, therefore, also offers the reader an opportunity to look at that information and the ideas noted above in a more detailed fashion. It places early childhood experiences and development within a neurological framework and connects this with new ideas related to learning, development and the future lives of children. That being said, there are some important points to consider before examining the research.

First, what we know about the brain is minute compared to what we don't know. Advances in technology and science have taught us a great deal but they have also told us that there is so much more to discover. Therefore, it is important to keep in mind that this book, like so many others related to the brain, is fluid and the information presented will likely change in the future as technology and research uncover more about the brain. This book is not about declaring any absolute 'truths' or certainties. Instead, it looks at what we know now based on the research available and it is written in a reader-friendly manner so that the research is accessible to anyone interested in nurturing a healthy mind.

Second, while this book adopts a broad scientific perspective, it also acknowledges that human development is a product of both nature and nurture. Neuroscience is offering us evidence of the connection between our genetic makeup, our predetermined neural capacities and the role of the environment in shaping our brain and, by association, our behaviour, intellect, emotions and social wellbeing. The development of a human brain begins before birth, continues into our twenties, and it carries on remodelling itself as we get older, and is influenced by both genetics and experience.

Third, this book follows similar works done by the author, which focused on the specific development of boys and girls. Not unlike those volumes, this book makes some significant acknowledgements to the work of so many others who have helped shape our understanding of child development and children's experiences of growing up, while framing the position of the author. As a white middle-class male, I openly acknowledge that the following pages may contain some bias and naivety as I attempt to merge neuroscience with the day-to-day experience of infancy, toddlerhood and early childhood. My background is such that I offer a certain perspective born out of research and a passion for enhancing the 'life worlds' and educational experiences of children. My hope, therefore, is that as you read through this book, you bear in mind that the ideas presented are a genuine attempt to link what neuroscience is telling us about how the brain develops, how our early life experiences can have lifelong implications, and the proactive measures that may be undertaken to ensure we are doing the best we can for all children at home and in school.

In developing my own theoretical and philosophical position, I have also drawn on the work of a number of authors and experts across a range of disciplines to help facilitate a better understanding of early childhood. I am not an early childhood practitioner but an educator of early childhood teachers and someone who has researched how the brain develops and the links between neural maturation, behaviour and learning. I also believe that we cannot understand our children's minds, behaviour and learning until we understand the structures and processes of their brains. As such, I am obliged to draw on the work of a number of authors and specialists, each of whom is duly noted throughout this book. I am also obliged to acknowledge that you, the reader, will have your own experiences and expertise to draw on and so should take what you can use while discarding those ideas with which you might disagree.

It is also significant to note that within our society, and indeed across all societies, the environments in which children are raised are not uniform. Race, class, culture, geography and socio-demographics, among other factors, will impact upon a child's development and life chances and, as such, it is beyond the scope of this work to completely articulate the multiple complexities that exist in a child's life. Rather, I acknowledge that childhood experiences are contextual in nature and heavily influenced by the realities of life. Moreover, there is already an excellent array of research and literature available to those who wish to explore the socio-cultural influences which shape child development.

By acknowledging the important role of the environment one might ask why it is significant to look at neuroscience and how the brain develops. After all, we can have some measure of influence on the environment but we can't really change a brain, can we? Actually our brain changes every day and the most current research tells us that we can shape and change the neuro-architecture of an individual in the earliest stages of life, but timing is crucial and the environment, relationships and care provided to children will have a long-lasting impact on their ability to learn, their capacity to regulate the emotional part of their brain and their overall development. T Berry Brazelton and Stanley Greenspan, world-renowned experts in paediatrics and psychiatry respectively, provide an eloquent description of the link between nature and nurture in stating that:

> *Even though a child's unique biology (nature) may launch early parent–child interactions in a certain direction, modifying the child's environment by adjusting parenting styles (nurture) can influence the outcomes significantly. After all, a gene can't express itself, or have an influence, without its intimate partner — the environment.*

We must also remember that hardwiring of the brain begins in utero and continues from birth throughout many important stages of life and, as such, a blueprint for behaviour and learning is in place very early in children's lives. To that end, caregivers and educators will also impact on the neurodevelopment of children with their relationships and the environments they create for caring and learning. So yes, we can indeed influence the development of the brain and this is where *Nurturing a Healthy Mind* begins.

The first chapter sets the scene by outlining some of the newest research related to the brain and neurodevelopment. It offers an overview of some of the most significant findings since the 1990s which have changed our view of the brain. These findings are also changing our views on how to best raise and educate children.

The next four chapters look at neurodevelopment and overall development beginning at conception and continuing to age six. The focus of this work is on early learning and age six is used as a developmental end point, because much of the hardwiring and moulding of the brain has already taken place by that time. On or around a child's seventh birthday, neurodevelopment slows down or even plateaus until puberty takes over. During adolescence there is a second major restructuring of the brain, but this is not the focus of this book.

Chapter Six focuses on 'learning'. Its aim is to give the reader a better understanding of the biology of learning and those things that impact learning. This chapter also looks at the interplay between gender and learning, society and learning, and the monumental importance of play and self-directed learning.

Chapter Seven focuses on language and literacy development, while Chapter Eight looks at emotional and social development. Again, the perspective taken comes primarily from neuroscientific research but other disciplines are also used to give a broad look at how we can impact on these developmental capacities in a positive fashion.

Chapter Nine moves into our understanding of cognitive development (thinking, problem solving, processing information) and intelligence. The emphasis is on identifying the growth of cognitive capacities and how we understand the word 'intelligence'. Theories of cognitive development are mixed with the newest research to provide the reader with a detailed look at how our rational brain evolves and how the very things that we as adults take for granted in relation to higher order thinking processes are nowhere near completion in children.

Finally, Chapter Ten looks at the broad topic of raising and educating healthy and happy children. It focuses on drawing together the information outlined in the previous nine chapters in an effort to give the reader some guiding principles for enhancing all that they do as parents, educators and role models. While perhaps acting as a summary, it reiterates that the way we approach life as adults is set in place very early in our development or, as already identified, the things we do 'in the beginning' are now known to be more crucial than we ever understood. We know this because we know so much more about the brain.

Chapter 1

New insights into the brain

The human brain, then, is the most complicated organization of matter that we know ... it is certainly more complicated in organization than is a mighty star, which is why we know so much more about the stars than about the brain.

— Isaac Asimov, author and biochemist

One of the most interesting things about the human brain is the fascination that all people seem to have with it. I have heard children in Year One sing songs about the brain's dendrites to the tune of 'My Darling Clementine' and watched grown adults enthralled when provided with an opportunity to look at an actual brain. A number of stories have been written with the brain as a central factor in the overall plot, whether it be zombies acquiring brains to satisfy some bizarre form of dietary supplementation or the Scarecrow from *The Wizard of Oz* looking to enhance his humanness. Indeed, there is no shortage of popular artefacts focusing on some aspect of the brain, for there is a long history of interest in the brain.

The first known writing on the brain dates back to ancient Sumerian records from 4000 BC, where an anonymous writer describes mind-altering sensations after eating the common poppy plant. The Egyptians are credited with the first written account of the anatomy of the brain on papyrus used to document 26 cases of brain injury along with various treatment recommendations. And while brain studies ceased during the Middle Ages due to a church ban on dissection and the study of human anatomy, interest in the gelatinous mass of cells between our ears has never waned. Fortunately, information about the brain has grown exponentially in recent times and modern research is far less intrusive than in days gone by.

From the beginning of the 1990s we have learned more about the brain than what we have known since the first recorded writings some 6000 years ago. There have been phenomenal advances in the field of neuroscience, as well as growth in the research and literature on anything and everything about the human brain. Ideas and questions surrounding aspects of mental illness, cognition and learning, education, memory, behaviour, emotions and general wellbeing have been explored and old ideas have been re-examined due to recent advances in research and technology. Functional brain scanning — in the form of electroencephalograms (EEGs) and magnetic resonance imaging (MRIs) — has unlocked many mysteries of the brain and presented them to the public in many forms. Interestingly, and in spite of what we now know, neuroscientists believe that we still know very little about the brain. That being said, neuroscience has also given us new ideas about the brain and how it determines behaviour, learning and what we can do as parents to enhance a child's brain development.

As noted above, most people, regardless of age, are fascinated by the brain — particularly how it works and how it makes us so unique. Many of the things we take for granted, including how we move, how we speak, how we remember, how we think and how we think about thinking, are the very things that separate us from all the other species on this planet. With the advent of technology, earlier information provided through rudimentary scientific methods and intuition can now be supported by data and research findings. It is this information that is making important contributions to our collective understanding of child development, given that we can now watch a child's brain when it is thinking.

For neuroscientists and all other professions interested in the brain, watching the mind at work is probably the single most important advancement in neuroscience since the beginning of brain research. Imagine that while you are sitting and reading, perhaps while having a sip of coffee every now and then, you could see how your brain works to comprehend the words on this page and the mechanics of your emotions when you realise that your coffee is too hot. The availability of this type of technology has changed much of what we used to believe about what has been eloquently referred to as the 'three-pound universe' between your ears.

Insights into the inner workings of the brain have drastically altered our views on the machinations of the mind and, by association, our knowledge of child development. Not all that long ago many psychologists believed that newborn infants could not think and were little more than tiny beings capable only of the simplest automatic responses; in essence, they were carrots that cried. Science now tells us how very wrong those psychologists were and how much of what we are and what we do as dictated by our brains is shaped in the earliest stages of life and does not ever seem to end. As I write these words I am buoyed by some of the latest research telling me that if I continue to exercise my brain as I get older and through the work I have come to love as my professional persona, I am decreasing the likelihood of losing my mind to dementia or Alzheimer's disease. So you see we all have a vested interest in understanding as much as we can about the brain and this is emphasised when we are responsible for nurturing and caring for the minds of our children. To that end here are a few simple things related to the developing brains of our children we should, pardon the pun, keep in mind.

Firstly, it is now widely recognised that not long after conception the systems and structures of the brain that provide us with the capabilities to do so many of the things we often take for granted as adults are being shaped. In relation to this, science also tells us that the brain development that takes place before the age of one is more rapid and extensive than we previously thought and more vulnerable to environmental influences. In other words, our capacity to navigate through a world of experiences over the course of a lifetime is beginning to be shaped before mum and dad light our first birthday candle.

A second compelling finding from a broad array of research is that while many once believed that brain development depended entirely on the genes a person was born with, this is simply not the case. Brain development hinges on a complex interplay between the genes a child is born with (nature) and the experiences he or she has (nurture), especially in the earliest stages of life. Arguments about which is more prominent, nature or nurture, are useless in the minds of a growing number of neuroscientists, psychologists, anthropologists and sociologists. Heredity and the environment influence each other and human development is the product of both.

With regards to the role of the environment, where we once believed that the experiences that happened before age three were rather insignificant, we now know that this is not true. Early experiences have a decisive impact on the architecture of the brain and on the nature and extent of our capacities in adulthood. For example, there is now overwhelming evidence that a lack of appropriate neural stimulation (for example, experience, touch and interaction) can lead to alterations in genetic mapping and, consequently, the neuro-architecture of the brain. The brain has a tremendous capacity for change (plasticity) throughout its lifespan but this decreases as we grow older. Early experiences help shape the mind, especially in the earliest stages of childhood given that a three-year-old has greater neural connectivity and almost twice as many synaptic connections as his or her paediatrician.

Another change of perspective regarding the brain and healthy development focuses on relationships and, in particular, the earliest relationships in life. It probably goes without saying that most people are acutely aware of the need for safe and secure relationships for young children. Of all the species on the planet, human beings have the longest child-rearing period and children are exceptionally reliant on safe and secure relationships to ensure their survival. Interestingly, we now know that this goes well beyond food and shelter; indeed, the very interactions children encounter via the relationships around them directly affect the way the brain is 'hardwired'. For instance, there is evidence telling us that infants who receive sensitive, secure and nurturing care in their first year of life are less likely than other children to respond to minor stresses by producing the stress hormone cortisol.

In the earliest stages of life, high levels of this powerful chemical can impair neurological development and many aspects of normal brain functioning. Studies have identified children who, after having been exposed to chronically elevated levels of cortisol, experience greater cognitive, social and motor developmental delays than other children. Conversely, young children with a history of secure attachment are less likely to demonstrate behaviour problems when encountering stress. Our long-term ability to navigate through life's emotional storms hinges on the biological systems shaped through our early experiences. It is, therefore, important for parents to always bear in mind that the types of relationships and attachment we have with our children can have long-term neurological and psychological consequences.

In terms of the early experiences of childhood, even the contextual framework of what constitutes an 'early experience' is changing. Not all that long ago many people believed that learning began at birth, that an infant or toddler's brain was not as active as an adult's, and that children could only think abstractly once they entered puberty. From a neuroscientific perspective, learning is a physiological process that begins just after conception and, depending on the circumstances, a child's brain is as active or perhaps more active than those of the adults around him and full brain maturation does not conclude until sometime after a person's twentieth birthday. Much of this will be discussed in the next few chapters but, as an example of the first point, consider that about seventeen days after conception neurons begin communicating with each other as they respond to stimuli within the womb. This communication is generally recognised as the brain's innate design to 'hardwire' itself and the development of neural pathways is at the core of learning and development. Furthermore, the hardwiring of the brain is a complex mix of timing and stimulation and after leaving the womb a child's rate of hardwiring increases exponentially as he responds to the plethora of environmental stimuli around him, or more simply stated, as he 'learns' from experience.

It should be obvious by now that a child's brain is very active. By the time they reach three years of age, a child's neural activity is twice that of an adult's and it will generally remain that way through the first decade of life. Once puberty kicks in and a child begins the journey through adolescence, this activity wanes somewhat and is replaced by a process of restructuring that lasts until at least their twenty-first birthday.

At the risk of sounding repetitive, the experiences in the early stages of a child's life can have a major influence on the neuro-architecture of the brain and the adult capacities arising from the overall development of the brain. Sensory experiences in the womb, followed by those in the early years of life, determine how the biological pathways of the brain develop and function which, in turn, influences intelligence, literacy, behaviour, and mental and physical health. To that end, there is little denying that brain development leading to learning and behaviour takes place long before a child first steps into any type of formal educational setting. Studies also tell us that it is important to remember that a child's head is not an empty vessel waiting for adults to fill it with knowledge as was commonly believed and practised, particularly in schools, well into the twentieth century.

As well as garnering greater insights into how the brain grows, matures and operates, the last couple of decades of brain research have given us some very interesting ideas to consider regarding how we educate our children. Over the course of many generations, educational systems functioned on the belief that a teacher's role was to impart knowledge into the minds of their students. Even today, many children are the recipients of this type of 'schooling'. However, given contemporary insights into the neuro-physiology and psychology of learning, we now know that the brain is a very active mechanism, as are children, when it comes to learning. As a species, we are innately curious and harbour a desire to learn. We are, arguably, most curious in the earliest stages of our lives as we work on making sense of the world, not the accumulation of facts or figures. Children have actually been likened to scientists themselves for both tend to be very goal-oriented, inquisitive, exploratory, experimental and driven to meet various needs. An inherent danger in this comparison, however, is evident in the growing educational mantra of 'prepping kids for the future'.

A rather worrying trend in many western countries, which is often premised on 'neuroscientific' research, is the natural curiosity of childhood being replaced with an orientation towards academic achievement. It is not terribly uncommon to hear about children immersed in a wide range of 'enrichment' programs as a means to enhance school success and future prospects. Often when children enter formal schooling this is exacerbated by a plethora of after-school activities or extra tuition. It is not too much of a stretch to consider this as early résumé-building, and while parents want to enhance their child's future prospects, this type of activity is developmentally unsound and highly problematic. Furthermore, a common misconception among parents and teachers alike is that it is their role to make every moment a teaching moment. Often this is seen under the guise of 'enrichment' whereby children are inundated with stimuli in the belief that they are little learning sponges, ready to soak up all that is placed in front of them, or perhaps more accurately, on top of them. In Chapters Five and Ten we will uncover the pitfalls and perils of such activity but at this point it is worth noting that there is nothing inherently wrong with using serendipitous moments of reading, singing, playing and talking as teaching moments. The key here is not the content but the message — and all too often the message, which is profoundly disturbing, is that preparation for college begins in kindergarten. As you read through this book a great deal of evidence will be provided for the case that, in terms of learning and teaching, all too often doing more to young children may actually result in achieving less.

Before moving into the next chapter, which begins to look at how the structural features of the brain develop, there is one final point to be made in relation to new research linking the brain and learning. Historically, much of our understanding of learning, especially learning in schools, was premised on the notion that thinking, feeling and doing could be planned for as separate entities. Ask most teachers who were trained in the not-too-distant past about how they were instructed to develop lesson plans and you will hear that they constructed their classes with cognitive (thinking), affective (feeling) and psycho-motor (doing) objectives. Interestingly, they were led to believe that these important targets operated in isolation from one another. In other words physical, social/emotional and cognitive learning were separable and in the end cognitive or 'intellectual' learning was deemed most important.

The brain, however, is a dynamically fluid mechanism and not a neat and tidy filing cabinet. Children learn by doing, they learn through their relationships (social intelligence), their emotions (emotional intelligence), and by making sense of their world (cognitive intelligence). Importantly, many of the highly regarded attributes of the cognitive mind that adults take for granted are the last things to mature. For example, being able to think in a highly analytical manner is something that improves during the teenage years and fully matures sometime after that. For children, the emotional part of the brain ensures their survival, fosters or hinders learning, and needs to be a primary consideration in any discussion related to healthy development, learning and social wellbeing. The following chapter, which begins to outline the growth, development and structure of your child's brain, helps to clarify this position.

Chapter 2

Genesis of the mind

During gestation, the brain takes shape from the bottom up, with
the brainstem maturing first. By the time we are born,
the limbic areas are partially developed but the neurons of the
cortex lack extensive connections to one another.
This immaturity — the lack of connections within and among
different regions of the brain — is what gives us that openness to
experience that is so critical to learning.

— Daniel J Siegel, neurobiologist

'Honey, I think I'm pregnant!' I remember when I first heard those emotionally laden words. My heart skipped a beat as I went from elation to apprehension. I'm going to be a dad ... wow ... I'm so happy ... wait ... I'm also petrified of the unknown that accompanies impending first-time parenthood! We need to think about names, car seats, setting up the baby's room and putting our life on hold! Where do we begin? Time to buy some books and seek the advice of experts!

For many first-time parents the thought of having a child is fraught with a range of emotions and ideas not too dissimilar to those mentioned here. Books are bought, expert advice is sought and a tsunami of opinions and ideas roll in from family and friends whether requested or not. There is so much to do, and while nine months seems like a long time when you are waiting to leave on an overseas holiday, it passes quickly when you know a new life is on the way!

For the developing child inside the womb there is also a great deal of activity and change, for this is the first environment for human growth. A new life is in the making and about seventeen days after conception that new life will start an amazing journey towards building one of the most unimaginable things imaginable: the human brain.

For previous generations of parents not much was known about the development of the brain and its relation to the development of the mind. The last twenty or so years have, however, provided expecting parents with a greater insight into neurodevelopment. The following chapter looks at what we now know, with a focus on the earliest stages of brain development and the factors that enrich and endanger healthy neural development. It starts by looking at how the brain begins to form and generate neurons and why this developmental phase is related to maternal health and lifestyle. Specifically, there is an explicit emphasis on maternal health and wellbeing, given that this will directly impact on the healthy development of a child's brain and, by association, its mind.

After looking at the early stages of brain development we then turn our attention to the intricacies and idiosyncrasies of early synaptic development and the growth of the brain's neural architecture. The intent here is to recognise that the ideas of the past related to maternal and infant health need to be scrutinised and carefully reconsidered. This is due to the fact that not all that long ago what was considered as integral to the early stages of nurturing and care for a child focused on what happened *after* a child's birth.

Prior to the end of the twentieth century little was actually known about early brain development or the complex nature of neural connections that begin to develop only three weeks after conception. And while we are now garnering greater insights into early brain development, the available statistics tell us that expectant parents either ignore, disregard or are unaware of the important timelines, opportunities and milestones that occur when a child is developing in the womb. It is important to remember that much of a child's future is shaped before birth as the architecture of the brain begins to be constructed via the mutual influences of genetics, environment and experience.

The growing baby brain

For the past 30 years, ultrasound imaging has provided parents with scanned images of the new addition to their families. These computerised images are produced using soundwaves and, while impressive, they are actually remnants of old technologies. Today the latest technology in ultrasound imaging can document early brain development and tells us that a great number of things can go wrong with a new life in the womb if mum does not look after herself. The womb is the first environment of life and, as such, must be well looked after to ensure healthy gene expression and human development. It is in the womb where the intricate weaving together of nature and nurture begins to shape what we might call the mind and all of its habits, likes, dislikes, patterns of behaviour and personality characteristics. It is important to bear in mind that the brain is arguably the most vulnerable part of human anatomy during pregnancy and there is no measure of parenting with a more direct influence on a child's developing brain than the time leading to the birth of a full-term baby.

In order to better understand the intricacies and vulnerabilities of a baby's developing brain in utero we need to look at the various developmental stages that occur not long after conception. In fact, it is only around seventeen days after conception that *neurulation* occurs: the process where one of the two cell layers of the embryo starts to thicken and build up along the middle forming a neural plate that, in turn, begins to change. The neural plate grows parallel ridges which eventually fold toward one another resulting in the formation of what is known as the neural tube between 22 and 26 days after conception. The entire process is usually complete in three to four weeks and this folding of tissue marks the beginning of the development of a child's entire mental universe. As the neural tube grows and changes it gives rise to both the spinal cord and the brain. Any hiccups in this process could result in a range of birth defects including spina bifida.

Another important feature of the neural tube is that this is the area where neurons originate through a process called *neurogenesis*. Neurogenesis actually begins as soon as the neural tube forms and the production of neurons, the building blocks of our brains, is then rapid during the first four months of pregnancy.

Once formed, neurons then move to different regions of the brain and make proper connections for particular functions to occur. This migration of neurons occurs from the third to the fifth month of pregnancy and precedes a rapid process of cell death referred to as *apoptosis*. Only about half the neurons generated during the early

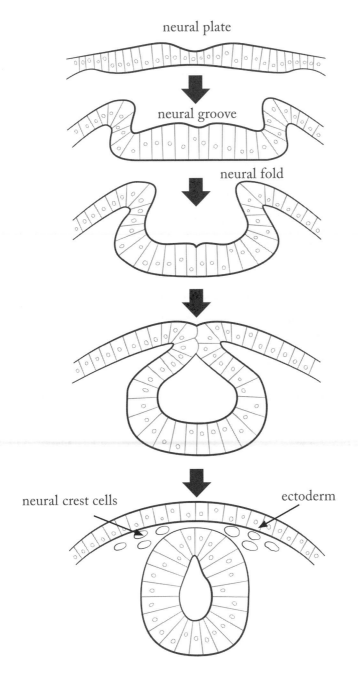

The formation of the neural tube.

stages of development survive to function in an adult. Scientists have studied various types of cell death for decades but the term 'apoptosis' was coined by former University of Queensland Professor of Pathology John Kerr and his research colleagues in 1972 when they identified and noted apoptosis as a process of programmed cell death. While it sounds rather ominous, it is a natural and necessary stage of brain development. In essence, the brain produces more neurons than necessary and 50 per cent of the neurons produced are then eliminated between six months of gestation and one month after birth. Interestingly, a related process, known as *synaptic pruning*, occurs during adolescence whereby the brain remodels itself by discarding unused synaptic connections. It is important to remember that both of these processes are perfectly normal and actually assist in making the brain more efficient, allowing for the normal and healthy development of neurons and neural connections.

In themselves, neurons are a type of nerve cell that store and transmit information to one another via electrochemical impulses referred to as synapses. Although this chapter provides a detailed look at the structure of a neuron and the mechanics of synaptic connections, it is important to note that the communication pathways neurons create could be referred to as learning in its purest sense. When neurons send signals to one another, as they respond to environmental stimuli, they create long-term communication superhighways which, in turn, shape the structures and functions of the mind.

During the nine months of pregnancy, the production and movement of neurons occurs at a rampant rate, averaging approximately 250,000 new neurons every minute. Once new neurons have finished their migration they begin to lay down the wiring that allows us to see, feel, taste, think and quite simply to aquire all the attributes that make us human beings. On the day when a baby leaves the womb, conservative estimates suggest that it will have at least 100 billion neurons which begin an amazingly rapid road to building new connections and extending the vast networks of those already formed in the womb. This is an important point to reiterate: even before the eventful day when a mother goes into labour and a new child is born, the brain will have been very busy making neural connections as it responds to environmental stimuli from inside and outside the womb, and the majority of the brain's basic architecture will be in place four months after conception.

As neurons take on the responsibility of being the brain's messengers, they are also responsible for helping to shape the brain's complex web of synaptic connections. It is significant to emphasise that the connections that develop do so via electrochemical impulses. In other words, the human brain consists of an intricate and unimaginable array of connectivity comprised of billions of neurons that do not actually have any physical contact with one another. This is arguably one of the most amazing characteristics of the brain and the fact that the brain's growing connectivity develops in an electrical sea of chemical transmitters tells us, that from conception, the health and lifestyle of the mother is critical — healthy mum equals healthy brain development! Studies tell us that the chemical imbalances in mothers who experience stress, poor nutrition and/or exposure to toxins during pregnancy will impact on the developing foetal brain.

There is no longer any doubt that genetic expression under the influence of poor maternal nutrition, alcohol use, illicit drug use and prolonged stress along with the consumption of caffeine, nicotine and some food additives may have long-term negative and potentially irreversible effects on a baby's brain. A growing body of research tells us that the possible intake of some of the chemicals noted above can directly impact on the developing brain long before the end of the first trimester. Studies also tell us that the foetal environment will have an impact on the formation of personality, tastes and abilities. For example, a baby's tastebuds emerge before birth. We know this due to research showing that something as seemingly insignificant as garlic in an expectant mother's amniotic fluid results in a child having a greater disposition to accept the taste of garlic in breast milk after birth. Worryingly, taste is not the only thing that can be passed on to a child. There is also a large body of empirical evidence stating that stress in the mother results in higher cortisol levels in the bloodstream and subsequently higher cortisol levels in an unborn child resulting in a range of physical and developmental difficulties pre- and post birth. Quite simply, the stress hormones produced by the mother slip through the placenta and can enter an unborn baby's brain. Maternal stress and stress in general has attracted a great deal of attention and, as such, is elaborated on later in this chapter and throughout this book. In terms of diet and lifestyle choices, it is important to remember that what mum eats or drinks also becomes part of an unborn baby's body and mind. Here are some examples of what we do know about some of those very choices.

Too much coffee can be a problem. While caffeine does not appear to cause birth or cognitive defects in children, there is evidence that women who consume large amounts of caffeine have a higher rate of miscarriage. Heavy caffeine consumption has also been associated with withdrawal symptoms in newborns. Currently it is suggested that pregnant women consume the equivalent of no more than 300 milligrams of caffeine a day, which is about two mugs of medium-strength coffee.

Given that caffeine can be trouble it should come as no surprise that nicotine is a bigger worry. Nicotine has been linked to an increased risk of miscarriage, and an increased risk of premature birth or low birth weight, both of which increase the likelihood of neurological impairment. Smoking has also been linked to decreased oxygen supply to the brain and the development of respiratory problems and facial abnormalities in unborn children. Worryingly, smoking and nicotine also increase the risk of sudden infant death syndrome (SIDS). The evidence here does seem to suggest that kicking or suspending the habit is not a bad idea when starting a family.

Along with caffeine and nicotine, alcohol also presents some concern. One of the most significant issues with drinking during pregnancy is foetal alcohol syndrome which may result in one or any combination of the following: the disruption of neuron development and neural migration; interference with dendrite growth and synaptic connectivity; cognitive impairment; impaired physical growth; impaired motor coordination; attention, memory and language impairment; facial or head abnormalities; and defects in the immune system. Aside from the potential problems noted above, alcohol also increases the chances of miscarriage, premature delivery and birth complications. It is important to note that numerous studies have identified an unborn child's brain as the organ most vulnerable to forms of developmental disturbance via alcohol consumption.

By now it should be apparent that what mum puts into her body may impact on an unborn child in a number of ways. Considering that something as natural as garlic can have an impact on an unborn baby's tastebuds, it should also come as no surprise that substances more toxic than those noted above are vastly more dangerous to an unborn child. Marijuana has been linked to premature birth, low birth weight, and an oversensitivity to various stimuli in the womb and later to stimuli in the environment after birth. There have also been reports of newborns of marijuana users experiencing severe withdrawal-like symptoms such as tremors and incessant crying. Cocaine and heroine are of arguably greater concern. Cocaine has been shown to alter the metabolism of some neurotransmitters (chemical messengers) and may impact on the structures of the brain that rely on these important chemicals. Other risk factors associated with cocaine use include premature birth, low birth weight, small head size and reduced blood flow to the brain. Heroin has also been linked to premature birth, respiratory complications and reduced head size.

While most of the factors noted above demonstrate immediate and overt problems, it is important to recognise that a number of long-term childhood maladies have also been connected to the intake or consumption of the substances above. For example, varying mood disorders, impulsive behaviours, cognitive impairments, sensory difficulties and psychiatric problems in children have been linked with maternal alcohol consumption and/or illicit drug use. In the end, the best advice for ensuring a good start to a child's healthy brain development may be to limit the consumption of the legal substances presented or perhaps completely abstain from the intake of the chemicals cited above once a decision to become pregnant has been made, or at the very least, once a woman discovers she is pregnant. Pregnancy is a very vulnerable time for the unborn brain and many things can go wrong, even in the healthiest of mothers. Remember, brain development starts less than three weeks after conception and in the greater scheme of things a potential lifetime of problems can be reduced markedly by choosing nine months of selected abstinence which, in turn, is likely to be healthier for mum, as well as baby.

For many generations people have known that the overall health of an expectant mother is very important. The importance of nutrition, for example, has been known for decades. Whatever mum eats or doesn't eat during pregnancy can impact on the development of the unborn child and this appears especially true after the first trimester when morning sickness and nausea tend to fade. This seems to coincide with the overall development of the foetus and, in particular, with the development of the brain, which is highly sensitive to the quantity and quality of nutrition it receives from around midway into gestation until about two years after birth. During this time there is a great deal of work going on in the brain of a child as it begins to lay down its neural hardwiring and, as such, the nutrients an infant receives prior to birth and in the first couple of years of life are very important. Moreover, numerous studies have shown that babies of malnourished mothers can have a range of problems early in life and throughout school where they tend to score lower on intelligence tests, have developmental language delays and exhibit more behavioural problems. In this regard it is important for expectant mothers to often consult with an obstetrician to ensure a well-balanced diet rich in protein and carbohydrates is being consumed, to meet the increased energy demands of both mother and baby.

Another important factor related to nutrition and foetal brain development is the role of folic acid. Folic acid is important for ensuring the proper development of the brain, skull and spinal cord and in reducing the risk of congenital heart defects, cleft lip and palate, and limb defects. Research into folic acid dates back almost a century and in the 1980s researchers found that low levels of folic acid could result in devastating brain and spinal cord abnormalities, including spina bifida. Since the brain begins to take shape about three weeks after conception, it is now widely accepted that when an expectant mum supplements her diet with folic acid, she greatly reduces the risk of abnormalities in overall brain development.

Notwithstanding all of the important nutritional considerations above, there are also a number of other factors related to healthy brain development in the womb. For example, during the earliest stages of child development the blood–brain barrier is very immature. The blood–brain barrier is a kind of membrane that surrounds and protects the brain, allowing only a few select chemicals to pass through in order to 'feed' itself. This important protective device helps to make the brain perhaps the most sterile part of the human body. However, while still developing, the blood–brain barrier is at an increased risk of neurological damage from environmental toxins. One of the most damaging is lead.

Most people are well aware of how toxic lead can be to the body. Lead is known to inhibit the movement of oxygen and calcium in the body and alters nerve signalling in the brain. Lead is perhaps the chemical of most concern given its historical use in commercial products such as paint and the questionable regulation of its continued use in products made overseas. Recent examples include the use of lead-based paint in the production of toys in China, which has seen a number of toys banned in western countries. Studies also tell us that maternal exposure to lead during pregnancy and/or low-level exposure to young children can be linked to behavioural problems, hyperactivity, impaired hearing along with potential reading and learning disabilities. And while lead poses the most immediate and well-known difficulties for mums and babies, other chemicals may also be problematic and it is probably best to avoid any environments where exposure to chemical compounds is possible.

Aside from the potential problems resulting from exposure to toxic substances such as lead, the last few years has produced some interesting, but as yet inconclusive, findings into the impact of food additives and exposure to electrical and/or medical equipment on pregnant mothers and unborn children. While many magazines might present arguments against mums ingesting foods or drinks containing aspartame or standing too close to overhead powerlines, studies supporting such proclamations have often been contradictory and indecisive. Perhaps a general rule of thumb is to remember that anything that might harm the mother will certainly harm the developing child. This is especially true when considering how the brain goes about setting up its myriad connections between neurons during the earliest stages of life.

The beginning of the brain's communication superhighway

As noted above, around three weeks after conception an unborn child's brain begins to produce billions of neurons that go on to form a superhighway of connectivity, which will result in mapping out the foundation of a person's behaviour and learning. Neurons are different from other cells in the human body and it is their structure and ability to transmit information to one another that makes them somewhat unique. Moreover, as neurons continue to emerge, mature and connect, the importance of their overall structure and functions becomes more apparent.

If you recall, neurons 'communicate' with one another through electrochemical signals. This communication occurs when neurons process information received from environmental stimuli. If, at this moment, a large explosion occurred outside your home, this information would facilitate a great deal of communication through various parts of your brain as you decided what action to take in response to the sudden noise. Importantly, the communication superhighway of the human brain is always active and changing as neurons talk to one another.

In themselves there are different types of neurons, but they all tend to resemble a bulb (nucleus) with sprouting roots or branches (dendrites) and a tail-like structure (axon). The dendrites act like antennae by receiving information from other neurons which, in turn, is passed on to other neurons via synapses. Synapses are the electrochemical impulses that occur from the axon of one neuron to the dendrites of another. These impulses need the assistance of important chemical messengers or 'neurotransmitters' to facilitate the overall communication process. Interestingly, different synapses are regulated by different neurotransmitters and thus neurotransmitters are like keys designed to open some locks but not others.

One of the most important characteristics of neurotransmitters is that they influence the activity, longevity and preservation of the synaptic connections and neurons themselves. They are integral to the transmission of information and the ongoing maintenance of the brain's neuro-circuitry. Moreover, the availability or absence of

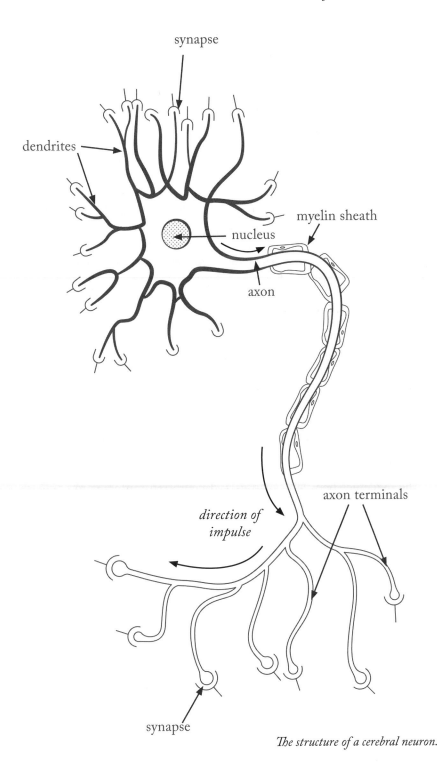

The structure of a cerebral neuron.

particular neurotransmitters influences all levels of brain activity. Neurotransmitters not only play an important role in neural connectivity, they also influence many aspects of behaviour: impulsivity, fidgeting and restfulness, along with thinking and attention, and feelings of slumber are all influenced by the chemical messengers in the brain. For example, the neurotransmitter melatonin induces sleep, while serotonin facilitates a feeling of calm, and dopamine influences motivation and novelty-seeking behaviours.

Although the science surrounding neurological activity is very complex, it is fairly well recognised that, at its most basic level, synaptic transmission occurs when our senses receive information from the environment around us and ask the brain to respond accordingly. The synaptic transmission of information is also the principle catalyst for developing long-lasting neural circuits. As our brains respond to the environment they lay down neural connections which, if continued and repeated over extensive periods of time, become hardwired highways for further signals to travel along. One of the easiest ways to think of the dynamics between synapses and neurotransmitters is to compare this with the activity of spark plugs in a mechanical engine. When you start the ignition of your car, the car will only run properly if the gap that exists at the top of a spark plug ignites, allowing for continued electrical surges and the overall firing of the engine. However, if any of your spark plugs are dirty or worn out they will act differently or may not operate at all, impacting on the car's performance. Generally speaking, this is what occurs through the synaptic transmission of information from the dendrites of one neuron to the axon terminals of another: continued firing results in continued hardwiring and the presence or absence of particular neuro-chemicals will impact on connections in the brain and result in different behaviours.

Aside from the structural and communicative aspects of neurons, another important component of neural connectivity and efficiency is a white fatty material called *myelin*. Myelin grows as a sheath around the axons of neurons and acts as an insulator and conduit for transmitting information from one neuron to the next. It is often referred to as the white matter of the brain and the thicker it is, the greater the speed and efficiency of neural transmission. The neural superhighway runs smoother when there is greater myelin and the build up of myelin, referred to as *myelination*, is rampant in the early stages of life. Myelination is a lengthy process resulting in the tripling of the size and weight of the brain, and does not finish until we are in our twenties, but in the early stages of childhood, myelin appears to grow in certain areas of the brain at certain times. Contemporary research suggests that it is during these times of myelination that particular types of sensory stimulation are most effective. This is one area where neuroscience has added a great deal to our understanding of learning and could help shape what we do with children in school.

Myelination of particular regions of the brain has been linked to the term 'learning windows'. In essence, the growth of myelin allows the circuits in these regions to work with greater efficiency and expediency, resulting in greater opportunities to enhance connectivity and, by association, to learn. Moreover, the overall process of myelination in various neural regions is specifically purposeful in location and duration. For example, the neural connections in the brainstem and in the major nerve areas running to the face, limbs, various parts of the abdomen and the organs receive substantive increases in myelin before birth and during infancy. This ensures that the connections necessary for a baby's basic survival (that is, breathing, heartbeat, sight) become quite efficient early in life. Other connections related to particular tasks or aspects of learning may have different timelines with regards to myelination and these will be explored in greater detail when we look at notions of learning in Chapters Six, Nine and Ten.

While myelin is an important factor in brain development, it is also significant to note how remarkable the brain is with regards to how it designs itself. As it continues to grow and develop in the earliest stages of life, the brain will form twice as many connections as needed, which results in an immensely complex web of connectivity. This overproduction is purposeful. If synapses are used repeatedly, over time they will become 'hardwired' pathways and part of the brain's permanent circuitry. Conversely, if they are not used repeatedly or often enough they are usually eliminated starting just after puberty through a process known as *synaptic pruning*. In other words, the brain overcompensates with the number of connections it produces to ensure the optimum number of possibilities for hardwiring and then gets rid of what it doesn't need. Moreover, the method by which the brain 'hardwires' its pathways tells us that the overall development of a child's neuro-circuitry is actually a 'use it or lose it' process whereby nurture helps to shape nature. In essence, the boundaries between nature and nurture are somewhat blurred during neurodevelopment in that experience plays a pivotal role in helping to 'wire' the innate structures of a child's brain towards behaving and engaging with the world in certain ways and this process begins in the womb.

Although the brain matures in direct relation to the stimuli provided by the environment, life in the womb is somewhat limited in terms of environmental stimulation. However, the womb's highly protected environment seems to be the best place for early brain development, given what we know about the number of difficulties that appear due to premature birth. Babies born at 32 weeks' gestation or earlier are at a greater risk of a number of maladies including, but not limited to: visual, motor and hearing deficits; attention problems; poor emotional regulation; and language delays. Therefore, the womb stands out as the first protective line of defence for assisting in the development of the circuitry noted above and in the early development of a number of important regions and structures within the brain. While the connective superhighway is being built so too are various systems and structures of the brain that not only rely on the information supplied through the synapses, but that also act as relay stations for passing on certain types of information.

Systems and structures of the brain

There are a number of ways to describe the complex structures within the brain that allow us to function as we do. One of the most common and reader-friendly approaches is to begin by looking at the brain's three principal regions and their main responsibilities: the *cerebral cortex* or *cerebrum* at the top, the *limbic system* in the middle and the *brainstem* connected to the spinal cord at the bottom. Within each of these regions are some important structures that also require some explanation in order to gain a better understanding of how the brain works and develops. However, it is very important to remember that while descriptions and diagrams of these regions of the brain might suggest that they act independently of one another, they are intimately connected in a web of complexity that unifies and influences each structure.

The brainstem is often referred to as the 'reptilian brain' because it closely resembles the brain of most reptiles. Many scientists believe that the brainstem began to evolve more than 500 million years ago and that it is the most ancient part of the human brain. Moreover, the brainstem is actually a collective term in that it is made up of a number of structures that not only connect the brain to the spinal cord but also ensure our survival.

When compared to other regions of the brain, the brainstem is relatively small, although it is dense with nerve cells and neural connections. One of the most important components of the brain is something known as the *reticular activating system* or RAS. The RAS has many connections with the rest of the brainstem and other regions of the brain and it is an important player in maintaining states of arousal and consciousness. The RAS is also intricately connected to the cerebellum, which sits just above the brainstem and just below the cerebral cortex.

The cerebellum (Latin for 'little brain') is a very important brain structure. The cerebellum has more neurons than any other part of the brain with some estimates suggesting that it contains about half of all the brain's neurons. The cerebellum is a very diverse and complex structure: it assists in finetuning the connections between our senses and movement and also plays a significant role in motor coordination. Interestingly enough, the cerebellum also seems to be a crucial component in the coordination of our thought processes. The cerebellum helps to explain why many people say they do their best thinking when they go for a walk; not only are they exercising their body, but they are also exercising their brain. This is also one

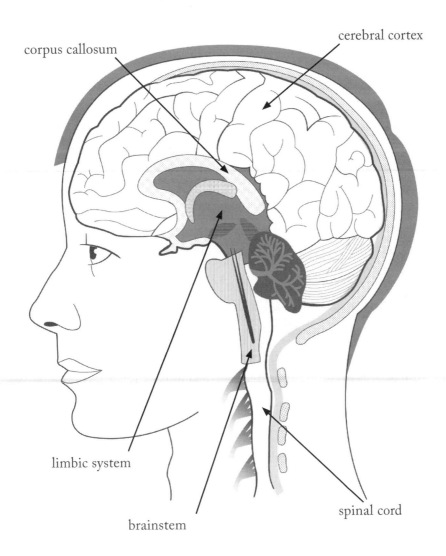

Principal regions of the human brain.

of the reasons that exercise, movement and play are so important for children, which I will delve into more later in this book.

While the RAS and cerebellum are important in terms of consciousness, thinking and movement, the brainstem is also the region of the brain where 'fight-or-flight' and other survival responses occur. Furthermore, the majority of functions not under conscious control also take place via the brainstem — your breathing, heartbeat, blood circulation, temperature regulation, tongue movements, vocal sounds, and movement of the muscles in the face and throat are all part of the brainstem's responsibilities. The brainstem also acts as a relay station for moving information around the brain but its most important link appears to be with the limbic system.

The limbic system sits above the brainstem and in the middle of the brain. The limbic system is often referred to as the emotional part of the brain, although that is somewhat simplistic. There is little doubt that the most vital function of the limbic system is that of processing emotional stimuli; however, it is also an important part of the brain with regards to storing and processing memories. Moreover, the limbic system also maintains crucial connections between the lower regions of the brain responsible for motor and automatic functions and the higher regions responsible for cognitive thought.

When fully developed the limbic system represents about one-fifth of the brain's volume and, aside from the functions noted above, it also plays a role in our sleep patterns, attention, motivation, regulation of bodily functions, hormones, the production of most of the chemicals found in the brain and initiating most of the many appetites and urges that direct us to behave in ways that usually help us to survive. In terms of behaviour and learning, four structures found in the limbic system are important to note: the amygdala, thalamus, hypothalamus and hippocampus.

The thalamus and hypothalamus help regulate vital functions of the body as we take in information through our senses. Any damage, trauma or injury to either of these structures can be life threatening. During normal development, the thalamus becomes evident in the first trimester with its overall function being to act as a type of filter or relay station by taking in various types of sensory information and directing it to other key areas of the brain for processing. The hypothalamus, while physically smaller than the thalamus, is no less important. Along with regulating bodily functions monitoring our heart rate, blood pressure, body temperature, the endocrine system and social–emotional behaviour, the hypothalamus also releases hormones in response to stress signals from the brain. Perhaps most importantly, the hypothalamus works in tandem with the pituitary gland to maintain *homeostasis*: the set point for normal bodily activity. For example, on a hot summer's day when we might start to stress due to overheating, the hypothalamus works to increase our rate of perspiration in an effort to lower the body's temperature and maintain homeostasis.

There is no denying that the thalamus and hypothalamus are very important for our wellbeing. However, they also rely on other areas of the brain to fulfil their functions adequately. Two of the most important structures that work in concert with the thalamus and hypothalamus are the amygdala and hippocampus.

In the last couple of decades the amygdala has garnered a great deal of attention and research because it is seen as the foundation of our emotions. There are actually two *amygdalae* but it is common practice to speak of them as a single entity given that they both perform the same function. Shaped like an almond (*amygdala* is the Greek word for 'almond'), early research discovered that the amygdala was primarily involved as a critical component in responding to danger and acted as the brain's alarm system. It performs this function by receiving sensory stimulation from the thalamus, especially stimulation related to fear, and sets in motion a variety of bodily mechanisms to ensure safety and survival. For example, when afraid, a person's amygdala is called into action by forcing the endocrine system to send out the appropriate hormones to raise the heart rate, blood pressure and to prepare the muscles for immediate action. If you have ever been unexpectedly startled, it would have been your amygdala that jumped into action and told the rest of your body to get ready to run or fight.

The amygdala continues to attract a great deal of interest and research. Recently, scientists identified another ingenious aspect of the amygdala's design linked to how it influences our behaviour and feelings. They discovered that different regions of the amygdala control certain emotions, so that when one part of the amygdala is stimulated, a fear reaction occurs, while other regions when stimulated may give you a 'warm' or 'floaty' feeling or put you into a fit of rage. Scientists believe that packing all of these types of mechanisms into one brain structure allows a person to shift from flight, fight or appeasement very swiftly when appropriate or necessary: if a smile doesn't ward off a bully or aggressor, then flight or attack is easily triggered.

As alluded to earlier, the limbic system appears to play a role in processing and storing memories and the amygdala is also part of this. The amygdala facilitates the consolidation of some long-term memories throughout various regions of the brain due to its capacity to label an experience with some form of emotional tag. Scientists

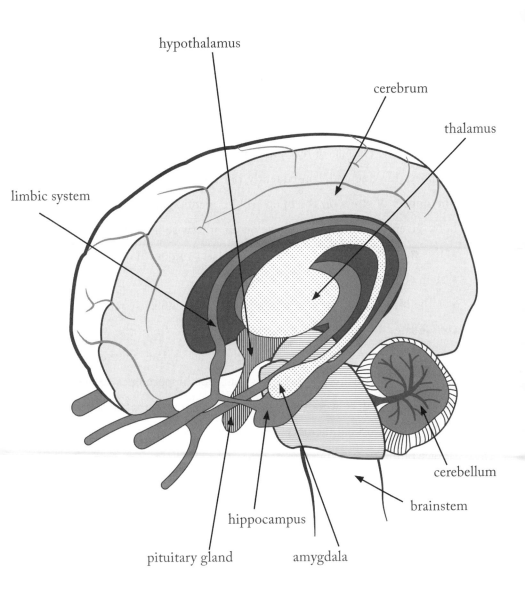

The limbic system is the processing centre
for emotions in the human brain.

believe, and research findings have identified, that the amygdala seems to decide what is important to remember by gauging its emotional intensity, and because it is very sensitive to fear, anxiety and stress-related incidents, learning can actually be impeded when the amygdala is aroused to engage in a fight-or-flight scenario. When we are in survival mode because of fear, prolonged anxiety or chronic stress, our memory, thinking and, consequently, our ability to learn, is hindered. The impact of stress on the brain will be mentioned throughout this book, given the impact it can have on an otherwise healthy mind, but at this stage, it is important to look at one last component of the limbic system closely aligned with the amygdala.

The hippocampus is another structure in the limbic system, which consolidates learning and converts information from the working memory to long-term storage throughout all regions of the brain. Located in both hemispheres of the brain, the hippocampus has been described as both a 'workhorse' and 'weigh station' in that it helps to facilitate our working memory which involves not only the temporary storage of information but also its processing into long-term memories. Taken in totality, the hippocampus helps us determine what might be worth remembering by looking for meaning from our past experiences and bringing the past, present and future together in a moment-by-moment whiteboard of the mind.

The hippocampus also works in tandem with the amygdala in that, while the amygdala attaches emotional value to an event, the hippocampus acts as a filter for deciding which information goes where. This filtering mechanism ensures we maintain our sanity by not having to attend to the innumerable bits of information our senses take in every second. This filtering mechanism is also an important mechanism for learning due to the fact that the hippocampus helps decide if something is novel or not and, if it is, we are more likely to give it our attention. The implications of this should be apparent with regards to school-age children. Learning experiences that are new or novel excite the limbic system, enhance motivation and are more likely to be stored in the brain's memory. Contrary to many individual beliefs about learning and to the dismay of *Star Trek*'s Mr Spock, learning is not devoid of emotion. Indeed, not unlike the connectivity that exists across all structures within the brain, emotion, cognition and learning are intimately linked, given how the limbic system reciprocally engages with our cerebrum.

Generally speaking, when most people think of the brain, or describe it, they use the cerebrum as their initial starting point. They are also aware that the cerebrum has a right and left hemisphere and have some understanding that it is this region of the brain where thinking, consciousness and many of our higher order thought processes take place. The most obvious feature of the cerebrum is its wrinkly surface which, from a design standpoint, is very purposeful. The cerebrum's highly convoluted structure allows for increases in its own overall surface area without increasing its volume or size. While every brain is unique and each individual maintains subtle variations in the surface landscape of the cerebrum, the cerebrum itself is similar in design and function for all individuals.

When looking at the structural aspects of the cerebrum, there are perhaps two fundamental aspects worthy of discussion in relation to their functionality: the four lobes that exist within each respective hemisphere and the nature of the hemispheres themselves.

The four lobes of the cerebrum operate in a vast array of neural connectivity between each other and the rest of the brain but, in themselves, they each fulfil some primary goals. The temporal lobes are located just above the ears and are responsible for processing auditory stimuli and for recognising danger and opportunities. They have also been indentified as the regions responsible for music perception and comprehension, higher visual processing, along with aspects of memory and language comprehension. The left temporal lobe houses an important area known as *Wernicke's area*. This particular part of the brain is composed of a number of smaller systems heavily involved in comprehension, in processing specific elements of language and in converting thoughts into language.

The occipital lobes lie at the back of the cerebrum where they appear to rest on the cerebellum. When you look at something, it is these important regions that process the information from the eyes and help you understand shape, colour, movement and depth. Interestingly, as visual information is processed through the thalamus, it is sent to the occipital region of the brain where it is matched with previously stored memories. It is, therefore, important to note that any particular visual stimuli you attend to are highly dependent on your previous experiences and several other brain systems.

The brain's parietal lobes lie at the top and along the sides of the head. The parietal lobes encompass a region of the brain known as the *somatosensory cortex* which receives and processes sensory stimulation. The processing of information related to body awareness (touch, sensations of pain and the position of the limbs), spatial orientation and awareness and some language functions are the responsibilities of the parietal lobes. The parietal lobes also allow you to grasp objects in that they provide the capacity to locate objects in relation to the body

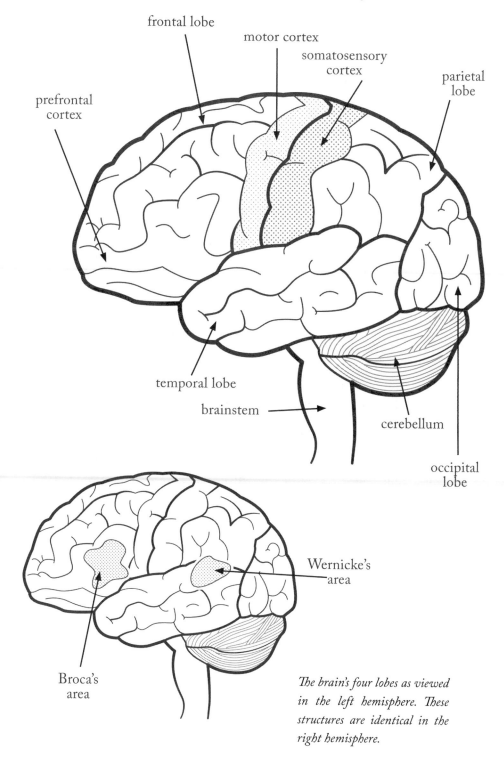

The brain's four lobes as viewed in the left hemisphere. These structures are identical in the right hemisphere.

and focus our attention on environmental stimuli. Simply stated, the parietal lobes allow you to touch and to feel the sensation of being touched, which occurs before birth and is perhaps one of the earliest examples of how we learn.

Notwithstanding the importance of the three lobes discussed above, it is usually the frontal lobes that get the greatest attention. This is due to the fact that for most of the neuroscientific world, the frontal lobes are regarded as the brain's chief executive officer. This crucial part of your brain allows you to be consciously aware of your thoughts and actions and to think about your thinking. This region is also linked to memory processing, higher order thinking, problem solving, planning, decision making, judgement, creativity and language. Not unlike the left temporal lobe, the left frontal lobe also assists with language. *Broca's area*, named after the French neuroscientist Paul Broca, is as important to our language capacities as Wernicke's area. However, unlike the comprehension capacities of Wernicke's area, Broca's area acts like the grammar and syntax centre by putting language together and providing the capacity to articulate thoughts through speaking and through the regulation of face and hand activity; we can speak and write because of Broca's area.

In terms of understanding behaviour and learning and overall child development the most significant regions within the frontal lobes worthy of detailed discussion are the prefrontal cortices. The prefrontal cortices coordinate and integrate most of the brain's functions due to their interconnectedness with every distinct unit of the brain. The prefrontal cortices serve many purposes. From thinking through one's actions or the responsibilities attached to those actions to abstract thinking to mediating emotional responses, it is the prefrontal cortices that separate humans from all other species. When you analyse a document, decide whether to have another glass of wine or restrain your anger, it is your prefrontal cortices that are busy at work.

One of the most interesting things to note regarding the maturation of the prefrontal cortices is that they do not fully mature until we enter our twenties. Current estimates suggest that the maturational journey is finished in women sometime before they turn 25, while for men it seems to take a few years longer. This is a very important concept for parents and teachers alike. We need to always remember that the regions of the brain responsible for survival and emotion are in full swing long before the regions responsible for logical and moral reasoning can follow suit, and, in the end, children will often rely on the emotional part of their brain to get through the day-to-day realities of 'growing up'.

One final note worth exploring on the structures and systems of the brain is its hemispheric makeup and the apparent lateralisation of many of the activities of body and mind. Long before researchers could look at a brain in action through current technology, there was plenty of evidence identifying certain functional differences between and across the right and left hemispheres. Much of this information came from traumatised brains. For example, those individuals who suffered a stroke in the left side of the brain would typically have difficulty with aspects of language and communication due to the fact that the language centres of the brain are predominantly housed in the left hemisphere.

Today, advances in brain imaging technology also tell us that the hemispheres of the brain are not simply mirror images of one another. One of the most interesting features of the hemispheres is that each one controls the opposite side of the body. If you were to wiggle the fingers on your left hand at this very moment it would be the right hemisphere that would be facilitating this. Importantly, while each side of the brain may have some particular responsibilities, they are intimately connected by a significant band of tissue known as the *corpus callosum*. This piece of neuro-anatomy is the only connective material between the hemispheres of the brain. While it is roughly the same size in males and females, it is proportionally larger in females due to the fact that the actual physical size of the brain is different between men and women; a male's brain is larger. As a result, some researchers believe that females have greater cross-talk between the hemispheres than males.

A second important aspect of the brain's hemispheres is that while some of the activities of the brain may be centralised in one hemisphere or the other, it does appear that in normal individuals no single mental activity is exclusively the domain of one hemisphere or the other. The overall functioning of each hemisphere does not happen in isolation from one another, nor does it happen without some measure of influence from the limbic system and/or the brainstem. In other words, you should carefully scrutinise any book, article or video suggesting you can build the capacities of one side of your brain while perhaps ignoring the other. Books professing such things are best left on the bookstore shelf, for brain lateralisation is still somewhat of a beguiling mystery for many researchers and, to date, the practical implications for teachers and parents are few. What researchers do know, however, is that each hemisphere appears to have decisively different characteristics or, dare we say, personalities. The left hemisphere is precise, time sensitive, used more when examining details, arguably pedantic and could be considered the analytical heartland of the mind. Language, verbal skills, logic, interpretation and arithmetic appear to be situated in the left side of our brain which is also concerned with details, details and more details. The right hemisphere, on the other hand, appears to be more holistic in design. Rather than seeking details and breaking information down, the right hemisphere is more involved with overall sensory perception, abstract thinking and the 'big picture'. Spatial awareness, geometry, nonverbal skills, visual pattern recognition and auditory discrimination have all been linked to the right hemisphere.

Finally, research dedicated to the hemispheres of the brain has also identified a number of differences between the hemispheres of males and females, including how the hemispheres process language, emotion and aspects of spatial awareness. Throughout this book we will look at research related to gender differences, behaviour and learning and this is done in recognition that recent neuroscientific research is telling us that from the earliest stages of development, male and female brains seem to differentiate themselves in ways that might impact on overall child development. Importantly, nature and nurture are not easily separated and any discussion related to the brains of boys and girls must always take into account the environment in which children grow and experience the world.

Chapter 3

When the brain leaves the womb

... when babies attend to something they seem to take in information about it and to be conscious of it in the same way as adults. When they see even a subtly unexpected event they show the same brain waves that adults do. They look steadily and intently at the event, their eyes scan the important features of the event, and their heart rate decreases in the same way. Every sign is that they are vividly conscious of the event in the same way that we adults are.

— Alison Gopnik, psychologist and philosopher

If you recall from Chapter One, prior to the advent of brain-scanning technologies, many psychologists and child development experts paid little attention to any suggestions that newborns could do much more than show reflexive actions to environmental stimuli. In the last two decades neuroscience has turned that position, if you will pardon the pun, on its head. Long before children can tell us what they are thinking we now know that, immediately after they are born, infants are using their brains in ways we had never known were possible. Their senses are soaking up massive amounts of information every second, their brains are learning from these experiences and their minds are beginning to mature.

From the onset, the terms 'brain' and 'mind' have been used interchangeably in this book. For a good number of scientists this is somewhat problematic and it is therefore important to clarify the meaning of these terms and to look at the subtle differences between the two. From this point onwards, any discussion related to the 'brain' generally refers to all of the structures, processes and responsibilities attended to, and processed by, the mechanics and physiology of the brain as an organ that separates us from all other species. The 'mind', however, is something that the brain possesses and uses and, as such, requires further explanation.

Ideas, philosophies and debates related to the mind, body and soul have abounded for centuries. This long history of uncertainty has continued and arguments about what the mind and soul are and how they relate to the body are still ever present and bewildering. In order to avoid being bogged down in a continuing philosophical quagmire, this book starts with a typical neuroscientific assumption that the mind is a product of the brain and that it is a complex set of faculties and attributes including, but not limited to, intelligence, consciousness, learning strategies, capacities to form language and the ability to think about thinking. In this sense, it is easiest to think of the brain and mind as intimately connected and when discussing the idiosyncrasies of either it can be assumed that they influence one another. However, a subtle yet important difference between the two is that the brain is also responsible for all other bodily functions.

At this point it also seems pertinent to note, once again, the intimate connection between nature and nurture given that, at birth, the brain is highly receptive to environmental stimuli. Even before researchers could look into the inner workings of the brain, it was acknowledged that demonstrating whether genetics or the environment played a greater role in the rearing of children by their biological parents was highly problematic, given how closely nature and nurture are intertwined. Growing bodies of research now support that the dance between nature and nurture is an intimately connected one and recognise that the exact interplay between genes and the environment may never be clearly defined. Nature and nurture work in tandem and any references to both will be made when necessary. Therefore, any discussion related to brain development are not those of nature versus nurture but rather how these factors interact and which may be more integral to various aspects of child development. It is important then to remember that when the doctor says, 'It's a boy (or girl)!', the brain of that child has a great structural foundation, but is still remarkably incomplete and will rely on the environment to help finish building one of the most complex mechanisms in the universe.

At birth, one of the most amazing characteristics readily visible is the sheer size of a newborn's head. Some textbooks have exaggerated this to such a degree that diagrams of infants resemble aliens rather than humans. It is the head that makes childbirth so painful and, when born, a baby's head is the largest part of the body and its brain is already one-quarter of the size of an adult's. During the first year of life the brain will triple in size and will require a great deal of energy in the form of glucose as it continues down its developmental pathway. Starting with the simplest circuits in the earliest stages of life in the womb, the brain begins to develop a complex array of circuitry via sensory pathways. Basic sensory skills like vision and hearing are some of the first to develop followed by early language skills and cognitive functions. Connections continue to emerge as a child grows and much of the strength and longevity of these connections depend on the experiences a child will have. However, it is important to remember that the brain is never a blank slate and every new skill is built upon previous learned skills. Therefore, while genetics map out the developmental trajectory of the brain, the brain grows rapidly after birth due to the abundance of environmental stimuli available and, as a result, early experiences are important aspects of healthy development. This is where nature and nurture continue to merge along the road known as *neural stimulation*.

The previous chapter identified that the brain is comprised of a number of structures which operate within a complex web of neural connections. These neural connections, in turn, are the product of electrochemical impulses commonly known as synapses, which are activated with the assistance of neurotransmitters. Working in a cyclical fashion, connections are formed as the brain is provided information through its senses and the connections provide the foundation for the brain to continue to mature, develop and act within the environment.

Synaptic growth, in itself, occurs rapidly and expansively during a baby's first year of life. A one-year-old child will have twice as many connections as its mother and the type of brain activity visible through scanning technology shows that its brain is far more similar to that of a grown adult than to its newborn sibling. It is also significant to remember that the brain is the only organ in the body that is incomplete at birth and the level of activity noted above remains high throughout the first decade of life. This suggests that children, especially infants and toddlers, seem biologically set up to learn. Another important factor related to the synapses and the wiring of the brain is the *action potential* of neural firing, which helps us to understand individual differences in children.

In simple terms, the action potential of a brain's neurochemistry refers primarily to a person's individual synaptic threshold when responding to certain environmental stimuli. For example, each of us will have different thresholds for the taste of various foods. For some the threshold for a red chilli is quite low and the unexpected consequence of biting into one for the first time creates a flood of activity in the brain. The tiny taste receptors on the tongue will send signals to the brain saying, 'Wow, this is hot!' This, in turn, elicits some immediate action (drinking water, perhaps), and also ensures that the experience is deeply ingrained in the memory for future references when encountering anything else that might resemble a chilli. Essentially what happens is that the experience of eating a chilli results in neurons hardwiring for the entire event, which can be called upon in a similar scenario when encountering new foods and potential taste sensations. If, however, a particular stimulus is too weak, neurons will not fire in the same way nor cross what is referred to as the 'response threshold' and in the end the action potential (or potential for neural action) is insignificant.

It must be noted that this is a very simplistic explanation given the unique characteristics of each individual brain and the complexity surrounding a person's own genetic makeup, physical condition and everyday environment. What is important to remember is that the various environmental stimuli children encounter as they grow impacts on their neural chemistry and any genetic predispositions or characteristics they have inherited. Developmental psychologists have long theorised about the important role of environmental stimuli for healthy growth and development. In an era of advanced technology and mind/brain research, neuroscience has added some valuable insights into sensory stimulation and deprivation.

Sensory stimulation is a very important aspect of neuro-development within the first year of life. The earliest stages of learning are not defined by a child's first days of school, but rather by a child's earliest experiences. When a newborn baby hears, sees, touches, smells or tastes something for the first time the brain sets about building neural connections of that experience. Repeated experiences will then contribute to the hardwiring of particular connections. This process could effectively be referred to as 'learning' and for any measure of learning to occur, the brain requires varying forms and degrees of stimulation. Conversely, the lack or omission of early environmental stimuli has the potential for lifelong difficulties.

The importance of sensory stimulation to the brain was uncovered by Nobel Prize-winning research conducted in the 1960s and 1970s. It was during this time that Torsten Wiesel and David Hubel found that depriving kittens of sight for a period of time immediately after birth resulted in various degrees of impaired vision or complete blindness. The methods used to deprive the kittens of visual stimulation is a bit too disconcerting to mention but what these researchers discovered was that, although there wasn't any evidence of physical damage to the brain, eye or optic nerve of the kittens during the experiments, sight was still impaired. This led the researchers to conclude that a lack of appropriate stimulation did not allow the kittens' brains to hardwire for sight. This work then led to similar research and conclusions in humans whereby children afflicted with congenital cataracts may experience the same outcomes described in the research with kittens if the cataracts are not removed as soon as possible. The researchers identified that when born with cataracts, regions of the infant brain linked to the optic nerve do not receive adequate stimulation and the development of the neural connections necessary for normal sight are hindered.

The work described above led researchers to believe that early neurological development is built on 'critical' or 'sensitive' periods for particular regions and/or functions of the brain. These 'critical' periods, in turn, require appropriate stimulation in order for normal development of the brain to occur. Importantly, scientists have recently found that sensory stimulation can also increase the overall number of dendrites on each neuron and that regions of the cerebrum or the 'thinking' part of the brain increase in size when exposed to stimulating conditions, and the longer the exposure, the more dendrites grow. For sufferers of dementia, Alzheimer's or other related mental illnesses, such discoveries are part of the emerging research into how a person might keep his or her brain healthy as they grow older based on the realisation that the growth of dendrites is not age specific but rather stimulation driven. For parents, this research not only demonstrates how crucial a healthy and stimulating environment can be for an infant but also that an environment devoid of appropriate stimuli can result in numerous long-term developmental problems and/or impairments. For many parents then, what constitutes an appropriate environment for brain development in the first year of life is an important question.

Most parents probably do not need to be told that a safe and secure environment with the requisite necessities of life, such as food and water, are the first important considerations for healthy development. During their first year of life, infants also rely on other important factors for healthy brain development such as the stimulus received through positive social interactions; holding and touching an infant literally acts as a type of brain food. Our understanding of these factors has come from trial and error and as a result of many generations of child rearing. Today, many of the positive aspects of parenting from previous generations are being increasingly supported by science and, in particular, by a greater understanding of the role of stimulation on the infant brain and the five senses involved in this process: hearing, sight, smell, taste and touch.

The five senses

The fundamental purpose of each of our five senses is to detect and discriminate between signals coming from the environment, which, in turn, is necessary for us to support vital life functions. All of our senses are present at birth but require stimulation in order to develop fully. Although all sensory stimulation is relayed through the thalamus, with the exception of smell, the processing of particular sensory stimuli does not occur in the exact same regions of the brain. If the neural connections for our senses were all located in same area of the brain then damage to the visual cortex, for example, would result in problems with the other senses as well. Fortunately, this is not the case and we now know that it is not uncommon for one sensory region of the brain to compensate for deficiencies in another. For example, individuals who have lost their ability to see often report that they hear better and have heightened sensations of touch. In itself, a baby's sense of touch is a very important aspect of early environmental stimulation and critical to healthy development.

Although not fully developed at birth, touch is one of a baby's most advanced abilities and, in terms of an infant's overall wellbeing, ranks just below oxygen, water or food in importance. Touch receptors develop in a baby's skin between two and five months after conception with the first and most numerous emerging around the mouth. This is one of the reasons why infants will explore so many things with their mouth in an effort to learn about the world around them. However, the mouth is but one 'touch' avenue for gaining information; babies learn a lot about their surroundings by touching things with various parts of their bodies and by being touched.

In itself, touch is actually comprised of different sensations that are turned into perceptions in a region of the brain known as the *somatosensory cortex*. When most of us think of the word 'touch' we are generally thinking of the 'cutaneous' sensation we get when our skin comes into contact with another person or object. However, the somatosensory cortex also monitors the sensations of temperature and pain via touch receptors in the skin. Touch is also

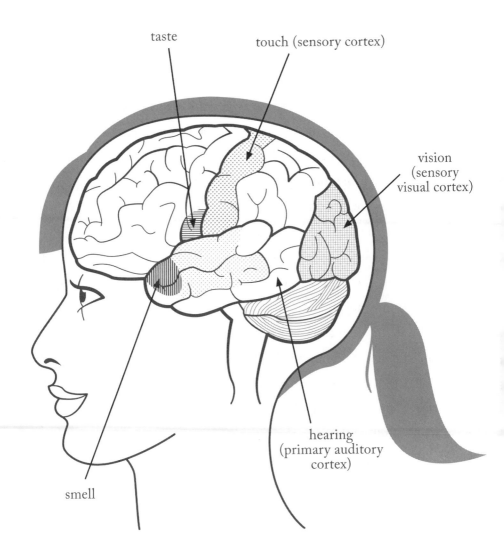

Location of the major senses in the human brain.

related to our innate perception of bodily position and movement. Known as *proprioception*, signals from the skin, muscles and joints tell the brain where our limbs are at any given instant in time. So while we might naively mistake touch as something that happens only with our hands, all of the aspects of touch noted above work together to provide us with a great deal of information about the world and, quite literally, about our physical place in the world. It is also worth mentioning that touch sensations help to shape the emotional life of a child.

When a mother gives birth, those who have helped deliver the baby work quickly to ensure that, notwithstanding any medical problems, the baby is given to the mother to hold. This is very important and purposeful in that the warm embrace between a baby and mother starts the building of the foundations of a child's emotional self. Premature births expose infants to a range of risks and a growing body of research has documented the beneficial effects of immediate skin-to-skin contact between mother and baby. Studies related to the touching that occurs between mothers and premature infants has identified that such tactile interactions can improve the overall health of an infant and can even shorten the amount of time in neonatal care. In some instances these types of interactions have even been linked to enhanced maternal milk production and various aspects of maternal health. Because of this research, incubators are now being designed to allow greater human contact.

At birth, touch sensitivity, not unlike the other senses, is rather immature. On the whole touch sensitivity develops in a head-to-toe sequence and improves with age as the brain matures. When a child celebrates their first birthday the neural connections in the brain are processing touch information four times faster than they were at birth, but the mouth will remain the centre of sensitivity for many years to come. However, while the mouth is an important source of information at birth and beyond, newborns also learn to take in information with their hands and are actively making sense of their world through touch. Some scientists and researchers have suggested that, when you watch a baby touch, you are actually watching the development of intelligence. As children grow and mature they continue to thrive on touch and physical contact and while touch is an obvious contributor to sensory motor development, it is also an important component of physical growth, emotional wellbeing, cognitive development and overall health.

Although touch is very important, during the first year of life the other senses also play an integral role in the development of a child's mind. Sight, hearing, taste and smell will all develop normally through the everyday interactions infants have within their home and any external environments. The human brain appears to have an innate and predetermined plan for the development of our senses and, as long as this map is intact at birth, it will continue to develop through experience. Parents and caregivers play a role in this process through the day-to-day interactions they have with newborns and infants. Positive early experiences that are nurturing, stable and predictable lay the foundation for healthy brain development. Talking, listening and responding to infant cues are important aspects of development and learning and help to shape ideas. At this point, however, what is interesting to note is the long-term impact that stress and extreme measures of sensory deprivation can have on a newborn.

Stress and the developing brain

As noted in the previous chapter, when the brain's stress mechanisms are activated it sets off a chemical chain reaction to ensure our survival. This reaction, from a physiological and neurological standpoint, is a very powerful force involving a variety of hormones and chemicals in the brain and body. Importantly, there are different types of stress and numerous misconceptions about stress and stressors. For example, people often say they are stressed due to being so busy or as a result of work demands and/or time pressures. For neurobiologists and stress researchers, stress is something we experience as an adaptive response to particular environmental stimuli triggering the brain into action. They are also quick to point out that not all stress is bad. Optimum levels of stress (eustress) will often act as powerful motivational and creative forces allowing us to achieve many things and complete many tasks. However, negative or chronic stress (distress) is potentially very destructive. If you play competitive sport you will rely on eustress to achieve your goals while distress is something you will work hard to avoid. In terms of better understanding the impact of stress on the developing brain, contemporary research has broken stress into three important categories: positive stress, tolerable stress and toxic stress.

Positive stress is best described as moderate, short-term increases in various stress-mediated biological functions (that is, heart rate and blood pressure) and is evident in children when they demonstrate frustration at not being able to do something or feel anxiety when adjusting to something new or novel, such as the first day at a new child-care setting. Positive stress is an important aspect of healthy development when it is experienced in the context of supportive and stable relationships, in that it enables children to develop and build adaptive responses to real-life situations.

Tolerable stress refers to those situations which could potentially disrupt brain architecture but are buffered by supportive relationships that further facilitate resilience and the development of coping mechanisms. The death of a significant family member, the impact of parental divorce, natural disasters, community violence and homelessness are prime examples of potential contributors to tolerable stress. While each of these will vary widely in terms of context and overall impact on a child, it is once again the support of significant adults in a child's life that is most important. Supportive and stable relationships help restore the body's stress response to baseline or normal and thereby assist in preventing long-term neuronal difficulties such as those seen in post-traumatic stress disorder or other mental health problems.

Toxic stress refers to the strong, frequent and/or prolonged activation of the body's stress response mechanisms and generally occurs in the absence of stable adult support and protection. Among the many things that might result in toxic stress, factors such as chronic neglect, recurrent physical and/or emotional abuse, acute maternal depression, extreme poverty and family violence are the most prominent contributors to this debilitating form of stress. Many studies now tell us that toxic stress disrupts brain architecture and contributes to immediate and long-term physical and mental health problems.

Stress has become a major health focus across much of society and this has been linked with the recognition that the earliest experiences a child has determine whether his or her developing brain architecture is provided with a strong or weak foundation for all future behaviour, learning and health. For example, it is widely recognised that children raised in disadvantaged areas or in an environment with low income and minimal parent education begin to score lower on many standardised developmental tests prior to their second birthday and that socio-economic status is one of the most reliable indicators of school success. It is also a well-known fact that children born into environments of abject poverty, neglect, abuse and/or mistreatment are at risk of early cognitive impairments and long-term physical and mental health issues. A great deal of evidence related to atypical child-rearing environments has been documented in studies of adopted children from institutionalised care. Children who have been the recipients of institutionalised care for extended periods of time have shown deficits and dramatic delays in cognitive abilities, emotional capacities, physical growth and behavioural development. Moreover, early experiences fraught with neglect, malnutrition, abuse and uncertainty activate the brain's stress mechanisms for survival and, as mentioned above, too much stress on a developing brain can lead to lifelong psychological and physical difficulties. It is therefore critical that the first twelve months of life take place within a safe and stable environment in order for healthy brain development to occur.

At the risk of appearing repetitive, the first thing a parent and/

or caregiver can do to ensure healthy development is to minimise stress. Above all else a baby seeks safety and security, and home environments devoid of stress are better suited for healthy brain development. This also means that relationships within the home environment are important. Children of all ages are exceptionally attuned to emotional fluctuations in the home due to relationship issues. Importantly, while sibling conflict is something that all parents work to minimise or remedy when raising a newborn baby, the relationship between parents is perhaps far more important. The need for caregiver stability appears so strong that the developing nervous system risks being adversely rewired from extended exposure to turbulent and/or troubled relationships within the home. Therefore, ongoing problems within relationships and between parents and/or caregivers need to be remedied as a matter of extreme importance.

The importance of nutrition and interaction

The next important factor for healthy brain development is proper nutrition. A baby's brain is highly sensitive to the quantity and quality of nutrients consumed. We also know that malnourishment prior to age two can result in cognitive difficulties, intelligence deficits, behavioural problems, sensory–motor deficits and slower language development. From a nutritional standpoint there is also a great deal of research noting that even after accounting for differences in socio-economic standing, children reared on breast milk appear to do better on tests of intelligence than those reared on formula. Studies looking at the impact of breastfeeding have identified that among the most consistent benefits of breastfeeding reported in developed countries is higher results on IQ tests and other measures of cognitive development among children and adults who had been breastfed compared with those who were formula-fed. For some people, attempts to link breastfeeding to cognitive development or intelligence are controversial; however, recent studies linking intelligence to breastfeeding parallel other studies, noting the positive benefits of breastfeeding to overall development and, as such, should not be completely ignored. Breastfeeding is not always an option for some mothers but whenever possible it is recommended that a mother breastfeeds her baby for the first twelve months of its life.

Finally, healthy neural development in the first twelve months requires plenty of interaction between an infant and parent or caregiver. This is not just about the day-to-day realities of care, hygiene and feeding, nor does it mean an infant should repeatedly be propped in front of a television watching a children's program promising to enhance a child's intellect via educationally designed activities. Instead, the first year of an infant's life is enriched by the interactions it has with people and most notably with its parents. The interactions between parent and infant are integral to social and emotional development, cognitive development and, in particular, language development. Before their first birthday an infant will have laid down important foundations for language and learning and much of this occurs when mum or dad engages in 'parentese' or the singsong-ey cadence adults use when talking to babies. The social interaction that occurs when parents talk and connect with infants has been shown to enhance cognitive ability, especially when parents engage in the form of rhythmic coupling that happens when they respond to babbling. How a parent responds to an infant's vocalisations appears to be a powerful mechanism for moving a child from babbling to fluent speech and the significance of the interactions a child has with parents and caregivers cannot be understated. These interactions, in a healthy, safe and supportive environment, help to lay down the groundwork for further brain development and learning after the first birthday.

Chapter 4

The toddler's brain

Your toddler's world is rapidly expanding both outside and inside. Being able to get around and to manipulate utensils expands his possibilities for discovery. The growth of language abilities improves his lines of communication. On the inside he is acquiring a sense of self-awareness, a greater memory capacity, and new ways of thinking ... keeping track of what is going on in a toddler's brain to make all these things possible is like trying to keep up with a room of lively two-year-olds.

— Norbert Herschkowitz, paediatrician and neurologist, and Elinore Chapman Herschkowitz, educator

'Keeping track of what is going on in a toddler's brain to make all these things possible is like trying to keep up with a room of lively two year olds' is an important statement given what we do and do not know about a child's developing mind. In the last couple of decades we have learned a great deal about the brain and the mind throughout the lifespan, yet there are still many unanswered questions. Some of the greatest mysteries exist in the earliest years of life when a child demonstrates greater independence and a capacity to move and express itself — much of this begins around their first birthday. Interestingly, as a child grows and develops, the mysteries of early infancy and toddlerhood also present many challenges to parents, caregivers and teachers alike. It is not uncommon to label these times of particular challenges as the era of 'terrible': the 'terrible twos' and 'trying threes'. However, as terrible as some days might be, a greater understanding of the development of the brain and mind may assist in qualifying those challenges.

As noted in the previous chapter, a human being's reliance on its parents for safety, protection and survival is lengthy and requires nurturing and loving relationships for optimum development. It probably goes without saying that even after their first birthday, a child will continue to need the type of positive environment discussed earlier to ensure healthy development. However, the needs of the child as they grow older begin to change in parallel with multiple aspects of development and, in particular, in relation to the maturing brain. This chapter provides insights into the developmental changes that occur from a child's first year of life to the day when they enter some form of educational setting, be it kindergarten or preschool. Important points related to brain development and maturation are provided, which are followed with the particular milestones children reach in cognitive, emotional, social and physical development.

One of the most important starting points when considering the developing brain is the growing importance of the environment on neural development as a child gets older. The environment includes the social, cultural and physical 'life world' of a child, and the interaction between a child and the environment is an integral and absolute requirement of brain development. This is particularly important when considering that while the number of neurons in the brain remains relatively stable after birth, the number of synapses increases markedly in the first three to four years of life and much of this results from a child's interactions with the world around it. In terms of overall synaptic development, it is important to note that the brain expects some types of experiences and depends on others.

The types of experiences the brain expects relate to the types of sensory stimulation it receives, whereby the brain 'expects' what we might call ordinary experiences to hardwire for particular capacities. For example, in order for a child's visual system to develop properly the brain expects to have opportunities to see things and this becomes much more readily available when a child leaves the womb. The auditory system is another example of something that will develop from the sounds the brain expects to hear after birth and this explains why ear infections in infants can lead to long-term hearing difficulties; anything that tampers with the internal workings of the ear will hinder stimulation. Many scientists now believe that brain 'expectant' stimulation is evidence that children enter the world prewired for certain abilities and all they need to develop these capacities is a range of 'normal' experiences. Every time an infant sees something, hears something, smells something, tastes something or feels something, its brain is rapidly building a network of neural connections that will become a superhighway for learning. As children grow and mature, the range of experiences they encounter continues to add to this superhighway until puberty kicks in and the brain restructures itself during adolescence. It is also important to reiterate that to deprive a child of such stimulation can impact normal brain development and this may prove to be irreversible.

In contrast to the experiences a child's brain *expects* to have happen, the experiences it *depends on* are adaptive processes that arise from specific contexts and the unique features of a child's individual environment. These experiences also add to synaptic connections and neural hardwiring and, in essence, are the things children learn as they engage with the world around them. Therein lies the fundamental difference between experience 'expectant' and experience 'dependant' processes: the nature of experience expectant stimulation generally applies to all children while experience dependant stimulation can be far more individualistic given the range of environments children are raised in. In other words, the experiences that the brain depends on could best be described as individual 'learning' experiences and an understanding of 'normal' brain maturation is important in terms of providing the most optimum opportunities for children in the first few years of life.

When considering that the brain depends on particular types of experiences to learn, some parents might think that they have to make every moment in a child's life a teachable one. Or perhaps, more worryingly, a parent might think that if a child's brain depends on some types of experiences for normal development perhaps a brain could be improved by engaging it in as many activities as possible. However, the provision of opportunities for children to learn from is not as complex or demanding as it might seem. After their first birthday children will continue to engage with the world in increasingly complex ways and in doing so they are actually 'feeding' their brains. Children take in a great deal of sensory stimulation through environments they experience and most environments are generally rich with stimulation. Unfortunately, some parents naively believe that if stimulation is so important, then surely more would be better.

One troubling phenomenon to emerge in many western countries since the mid-1970s has been the misguided notion that enriching an environment or 'hyperstimulating' a child might improve their intellect and enhance their educational future. For all the positives that have been uncovered, advances in mind/brain science have also seen the dubious use of particular studies as a mechanism for advocating educational tools and programs designed to give children a head start on the road to learning and academic prowess. Such prescribed roads to enrichment, however, are problematic on many accounts, not least of which is how the science surrounding notions of enrichment has been used.

Some of the first studies looking at enriched environments took place about 50 years ago. In the early 1960s, researchers found that rats raised in enriched environments had noticeable changes in some neurotransmitters in their brains compared to rats who did not receive such stimulation. Further studies found that enriched rat environments also led to rats having increases in synaptic density and connections as well as an increase in the overall size of the cerebral cortex. However, it is the term 'enriched' that deserves more attention here, rather than the actual outcomes of enrichment.

If you have ever been to a pet store that sells small rodents, such as mice or rats, you would notice that their cages had many things to keep them amused. Such cages might have those exercise wheels in them that allow animals to run endlessly to nowhere. They may have toys with bells that ring when moved or mazes with a prize at the end for those clever rats who can find their way around. In the rat studies noted above these were the types of enriched environments provided to one group of rats. The rats that weren't allowed entry into those fun-filled rodent amusement parks lived in 'dull' cages without any of the toys mentioned. It should come as no surprise then that the rats that were given things to do and play with experienced positive effects on their brains. What may be surprising to you, however, is that studies that have looked at rats in their natural environments full of the types of challenges that can only be encountered outside of any cage have even *better* brains than their 'enriched' counterparts playing with toys. In other words, toys and mazes do not a great rat brain make!

Part of the problem with agendas set out to enrich a child's environment or learning experiences is the word 'enriched' and its meaning. Too often 'enriched' is set against the term 'impoverished' and careful marketing can make many 'normal' homes seem like they are missing something or perhaps that they need to be improved in some way to ensure they don't sit at the wrong end of an enrichment continuum. To date, research suggests that parents should relax, as the vast majority of home environments sit somewhere in between the words 'enriched' and 'impoverished' and are more than adequate for normal healthy brain development and learning to occur. Furthermore, there isn't any reliable evidence to suggest that special stimulation or enrichment activities beyond the experiences in most homes can lead to some measure of advanced brain development. The term 'most' is used as a gentle reminder that children raised in abject poverty, trauma, abuse or other forms of chronic stress may incur a range of developmental difficulties. To that end it is useful to look at the types of experiences and environments the brains of young children need prior to the formal years of schooling.

One of the best ways of looking at the types of experiences that are beneficial for children is to focus on particular aspects of development as they relate to brain maturation. The types of development proposed are those found in many child development or educational psychology textbooks and generally labelled as cognitive, social, emotional and physical/motor development. It is important to note that from this point onwards each area of development will be discussed separately but they are not easily separated in reality. The brain is a highly complex mechanism and, while we can package aspects of development into neat little boxes in a book, for the human brain feeling, thinking and doing are intimately connected.

Prior to looking at each type of development, it is important to reiterate that before a child reaches their fourth birthday, there has already been a great deal of activity and development in their brain. Much of this development occurs through increases in myelin and via synaptic growth and refinement. Parents see the evidence of such development through the dramatic shifts in abilities and comprehension that their children demonstrate as each month passes. From babbling to talking, and from crawling to walking, children change quickly and often without much notice. These shifts can be characterised as the product of learning and there are some points to bear in mind when considering when these changes occur.

First, all aspects of development are the result of an intricate dance between maturation and learning or nature and nurture. As they grow older, children also become more personally active in progressing their overall development through a cumulative process increasingly influenced by the world around them. The importance of relationships and interacting with the world has already been discussed, but it is also crucial in terms of the links between overall development and nutrition, safety and movement.

What to feed the young brain

Proper nutrition is perhaps the first priority for healthy brain development. There exists a large body of research telling us that a developing brain is more vulnerable to poor nutrition or nutrient insufficiency and that certain nutrients in some foods have greater effects on brain development than others. For example, iron is an incredibly important mineral with regards to myelination and the development of particular regions of the hippocampus — the part of the brain responsible for aspects of memory. Science also tells us that the nutrient requirements of the brain are expansive, considering how the brain develops and how much energy it uses and, as such, children must receive a diet that is diverse in content and nutritionally rich. It is also worth noting that, not unlike the marketing of toys to improve the brain, the marketing of food or food supplements as brain enhancers has seen an increase in advertising pressure aimed at unsuspecting parents. To help alleviate any concerns and keep things in perspective, here are four points that will ensure the brain is properly nourished:

- Forget any brain-boosting supplements suggesting that they will make children smarter. Instead, rely on commonsense: the best brain boosters can be found through eating more vegetables and lessening the intake of simple sugars.
- Foods rich in antioxidants help 'clean' the mind and body and include things like sultanas, berries, apples, grapes, cherries, prunes and spinach (while the last two foods may not be high on a child's preferred food list, the others offer a range of snacks that usually meet the approval of young tastebuds).

- Omega-3 fatty acids are important and can be found in many types of seafood. Flaxseed oil and walnuts are also high in omega-3 fatty acids but for children with either an allergy or an aversion to nuts or seafood, it is also possible to purchase special breads, eggs or milks enriched with omega-3.

- The brain and body requires a great deal of energy to run and much of that energy comes from carbohydrates. However, too many simple carbohydrates, such as white bread, sugar, soft drinks and fruit, are problematic in that they can create a sharp rise in blood sugar. Complex carbohydrates, on the other hand, break down over longer periods of time and do not cause such sharp rises in blood sugar. Complex carbohydrates can generally be found in wholegrains and foods made with grains; starchy vegetables, such as corn and potatoes; and legumes.

Aside from making sure children have adequate and proper nutrition to ensure healthy brain development, safe, secure, predictable, stable and loving environments are also important aspects of that development. In the early years of life the brain's fundamental concern and focus is survival, not learning. A child's survival instincts and the mechanisms of the brain programmed to recognise threats and adversity mature long before the regions of their brain responsible for higher order thinking and abstract thought come into line. When sensing danger or feeling under threat the brain can revert to the types of stress responses discussed in the previous chapter. And as noted earlier, chronic stress or 'toxic' stress is a blueprint for long-term difficulties in all areas of development. The brain's preoccupation with survival tells us that an environment of safety and security is the best context for healthy development and learning in the first few years of life.

Finally, with its nutritional and survival needs met, the brain also thrives on environments that allow for plenty of movement. In a cyclical fashion, as a child's muscles grow and strengthen, the child becomes more physically active in the world around them which in turn enhances overall brain development and greater physical activity. The development of gross and fine motor skills are a critical part of learning about the social and physical world and an environment that safely allows for all aspects of movement is one that enhances all aspects of development.

Sitting still is not the best option for a child

The development of a child's physical abilities — and, indeed, many of the regions of the brain that facilitate motor movement — is a relatively slow process in humans compared to other mammals. Part of the reason behind this is that the regions of the human brain responsible for movement are incredibly complex. Moreover, a great proportion of the learning a child experiences occurs via its senses and in the first year or so much of the information infants receive is a one-way street of sensory stimulation and interpretation. The motor circuits of the brain require tremendous amounts of feedback from the world and as a child grows and begins to move about, the pace of neuromuscular development sets important limits on when various motor skills are available to each child. It is also worth stating that while muscles are growing, so too is myelin, which will help improve the communication between the motor regions of the brain, allowing for faster and more efficient communication between those brain regions and the muscles in the legs and hands.

Myelin growth is critical in terms of movement. Areas of the brain that connect the variety of nerve fibres that facilitate motor development will generally undergo a great deal of myelin growth between the first and second years of life and along with this parents will see their child go from not being able to sit on their own to walking, exploring the world and opening cupboards that were once in their child's too-hard basket. Of course, some children will become mobile sooner than others but it is important to remember that the progression from sitting to crawling to walking is a natural one with general timeframes and can be quite different for each child within a family and between other families.

In terms of physical development and movement, the progression of physical development occurs from the inner part of the body to the outer parts and from head to toe. Generally speaking, as the brain matures and gains greater information about the environment, parents will see improvements in their child's fine and gross motor skills, although gross motor skills are evident earlier in life.

A person's gross motor skills involve large muscle groups of the trunk and limbs and whole body movements such as rolling, jumping, throwing and running. One of the first signs of improved gross motor skills appears when an infant rolls over on its own for the first time. The types of spontaneous activities that occur between parents and toddlers contribute to a child's motor-skill development as gross motor skills, strength, coordination and balance are interrelated. Fine motor skills, on the other hand, are those that require the small muscles of the mouth, arms and hands to work together to perform precise and refined movements. Fine motor skills are visible when a child holds its first rattle, although the immature nature of those skills can result in rattle-inflicted head wounds! Fine motor skills involve deliberate and controlled movements that not only require muscle development but also maturation of the central nervous system in order for such refined skills to improve. In regards to long-term developmental goals across a range of abilities, gross motor systems play an important role in children's exploratory behaviours, playground activities and athletics while fine motor systems are more important for learning to read and write.

Generally speaking, fine and gross motor skills develop in a sequential manner, although the pace of such development is uneven, characterised by rapid spurts and different for every child. Parents need look no further than any playground to see evidence of the variation in gross and fine motor skills among children of the same age. That being said, and excluding any form of developmental impairments, the vast majority of children achieve the same gross and fine motor milestones at very similar ages within a predictable pattern and sequence. The table on the following pages offers a list of such motor milestones and the respective ages of each milestone parents can expect to see before their child reaches their fourth birthday. It is, however, important to emphasise that the milestones noted in the table represent *average* ages; there will be individual differences regarding the precise age at which every child achieves each milestone.

Average age milestone achievement	Fine motor milestones	Gross motor milestones
1–6 months of age		
1–2 months	• Most actions are reflexive • Reaching for objects is ineffective	• Movements of the arms, legs and body are random and often jerky • Able to lift chin slightly • The head is wobbly while sitting and neck muscles are weak
2–4 months	• Can grasp some things depending on weight of object (i.e. baby rattle)	• Strength in neck improves and, as a result, a child also begins to raise and hold head steady in sitting • Rolls from back to side and from tummy to side • Puts weight on arms while on tummy (tummy time) • Sits on propped arms
4–6 months	• Begins to reach and grasp and demonstrates greater control with these movements	• Rolls from tummy to back and back to tummy • Can sit in a highchair • Wiggles a few feet forward • Pushes up with arms while on tummy and sits propped on hands • Is able to sit briefly on its own
7–12 months of age		
6–8 months	• Can grasp objects with thumb and forefinger (pincer grip) • Can put objects in containers and can take them out	• Can sit unsupported for 30 seconds or more • Rocks on all fours • Pivots in a circle while on tummy and reaches while on tummy • Transitions from tummy to sitting • Begins to crawl forward

Average age milestone achievement	Fine motor milestones	Gross motor milestones
8–10 months	• Can clasp hands	• Transitions from tummy to sitting and from sitting to tummy • Pulls to stand while holding on • Creeps forward on all fours • Can stand while leaning on furniture
10–12 months	• Releases objects unsophisticatedly • May hold crayon or chalk and try to scribble • Points with index finger	• Moves with greater fluidity and confidence using furniture as support (cruising) • Can briefly stand unsupported • Can transfer between sitting and crawling • Will begin to make first independent steps • Assumes/maintains kneeling
1–3 years of age		
12–18 months	• Can stack objects • Can hold two or three objects in one hand • Can roll ball to others and pick up objects in motion • Can unzip zippers • Can take apart toys and put them back together • Can drink from a cup, brush hair and scribble with a crayon • Around 18 months of age a child begins to demonstrate controlled release of objects	• Can walk independently • Begins to creep up stairs and will gradually walk up stairs with help • Will try to climb out of highchair • Squats to play • Kneels • Can stoop over and recover • Can walk in circles and backwards • Tries to kick balls • Climbs on furniture • Pulls toy while walking

Average age milestone achievement	Fine motor milestones	Gross motor milestones
18–24 months	• Continued improvements in fine motor tasks are evident • Can grasp and release a range of objects with greater control • Begins to show hand preference • May put on shoes but often on the wrong foot • May draw a circle if shown how	• Can run and jump in place • Kicks a stationary ball • Can walk up stairs independently • Can throw a ball overhand • Can propel 'ride-on' toys forward
24–36 months	• Better coordination of movements of the wrist, fingers and palms • Can unscrew lids and unwrap paper • Can use small scissors • Can rotate jigsaw pieces and complete a simple puzzle	• Can hop on one foot • Walks more rhythmically • Can walk up and down stairs, alternating feet • Can walk backwards • Can briefly balance on one foot • Can throw overhand at a target • Can catch a rolled ball • Can ride a tricycle using pedals

It is obvious that as a child reaches the various motor milestones outlined in the table, they gain greater independence and capacities for engaging with the world around them. Motor-skill development is also important with regards to the brain's vestibular system and cerebellum, two other significant structures of the brain. The vestibular system is a very complex sensory system that continually bombards the brain with information to assist in balance, spatial orientation, visual gaze, movement and maintaining head and body posture. And as noted earlier, the cerebellum is the region of the brain responsible for a number of functions linked to motor coordination, movement and cognition. Importantly, as children's motor skills mature and improve, they not only exercise the body but also exercise the vestibular system and the cerebellum. This is one reason why, as appealing as it might be for children to sit still, they often won't and possibly shouldn't as their brain calls out for movement to exercise the mind as well as the body. Interestingly, advancements in strength and the sophistication of movements and motor skills mirror increased milestones in many cognitive capacities.

Improved cognition and growing intelligence

Compared to watching the physical changes associated with age, watching the cognitive capacities of a child's mind is not as easily done. This is exacerbated by the fact that adults easily take many aspects of their own cognitive abilities for granted and forget that the developing brain and mind of a child is quite different to their own. Our use of the memory systems of the brain, along with our capacities for abstract and analytical thinking, among many other components of higher cognitive processes, are only beginning to develop in toddlers. Even in an era of presumably advanced mind/brain science, there are still a large number of mysteries around various aspects of cognitive development and the unfolding of the mind. We do, however, have some greater insights into what to expect with regards to cognitive development during toddlerhood and perhaps the most appropriate place to begin that discussion is with defining what 'cognition' might entail.

Currently there are a number of scientific fields that study cognition in and of the human brain and with that comes diverse explanations of what cognition might actually mean. In the context of this book, cognition refers to the mental activities of the mind that allow us to acquire and manipulate knowledge. As yet, researchers are not able to directly observe how a three-year-old brain forms ideas and thoughts. However, years of research using child observations coupled with contemporary insights into the brain are providing an expanding array of information related to the inner workings of a young mind. In terms of overall cognitive development, for example, we do know that the brain is changing extensively and rapidly prior to a child's fourth birthday, which allows it to engage in increasingly complex cognitive processes. As noted earlier, we also know that in the early stages of life the brain is actively creating a vast and complex array of neural connections as it responds to environmental stimuli and that myelination continues to advance and enhance overall neural connectivity. From one year of age, a child will reach a number of other cognitive milestones related to the brain's structures and functions and these become increasingly evident through a child's behaviour and actions.

One of the first things parents will notice in relation to cognitive development is an improvement in aspects of memory. Toddlers will demonstrate greater capacities at remembering familiar faces and where they might have placed a toy. Moreover, various structural aspects related to a number of important regions in a child's brain undergo some significant modifications. Specifically, synaptic connections between the hippocampus, neocortex (the outer layer of the cerebrum) and the limbic system become stronger and with this so too does the emergence of specific aspects of memory. It is important, however, to remember that even adult versions of memory are prone to error and because it takes a significant amount of time for memory to improve, children will not have the same short-term or long-term memory capacities as their parents. This is one of the reasons why children will quickly forget where they may have put your mobile phone and why, as adults, we have difficulty recalling events from our own childhood before the age of four of five. In one of life's bittersweet ironies, our memory improves as we grow older but it is also one of the things that begin to diminish as we reach old age. In one sense we could say that the cognitive aspects of our memory shift from childhood to adulthood and back to childhood.

While a child's memory capacities improve as a product of neurological maturation, so too does the communication between the hemispheres of the brain via the corpus callosum. Synaptic connections between the hemispheres improve, as does synaptic density between the regions of the brain related to language and reading, allowing for increased language skills, improved vocabulary and the emergence of some higher order thinking skills. There is also evidence of increased connectivity between the regions of the brain responsible for language comprehension, syntax and reading. This increased connectivity results in an explosion of language abilities somewhere around a child's third year. Generally speaking, from roughly one to three years of age a child will demonstrate marked increases in vocabulary, sentence structure, grammar and general communication but at three years of age these increases are dwarfed by the range of vocabulary and adult-like sentences now articulated with increasing ease and without specific instruction.

The emergence of language, improved memory and higher order thinking at the intersection of new experiences and increased engagement with the environment is often linked with notions of intelligence. As the brain matures with its superhighway of interconnectivity and increased myelination, it becomes faster and far more efficient. A greater number of connections and greater amounts of myelin equal greater neural speed and efficiency which, in turn, contribute to a child's overall intelligence. Importantly, connectivity and myelination are not restricted to one area of the brain and, thus, intelligence, unlike many other cognitive functions, is not something to be found in one region of the brain. As noted earlier, we do know that many of our most sophisticated mental abilities are mediated and processed through our prefrontal cortices, including maintaining attention, mediating emotions, empathising, analytical thinking and decision making. It should not be surprising then, that as the prefrontal cortices mature, children may appear more intelligent given that they will be better able to demonstrate improvements in attention, concentration, memory, language, planning, analytical skills and numerous other capacities. It should also not be surprising that, given the full maturation of the prefrontal cortices does not happen until we reach our twenties, young children will rely a great deal on the emotional part of their brain for survival, learning and getting what they want or need.

Surviving, learning and relating — the keys to emotional and social development

Most parents are acutely aware that emotions tend to dominate the behaviour and lives of children, and first-time parents learn this lesson very quickly! Young children can quite rapidly move from smiling to crying to lashing out and often without any advance warning. Part of the reason for this was alluded to earlier and concerns the survival instincts of the brain but much of this is also due to brain maturation where the first three years see significant changes in regions responsible for emotional functioning and processing. How parents and the adults around children respond to emotional events can have profound impacts on many aspects of brain development and it is therefore important to understand what contributes to emotional and social development in toddlers. A good starting point is to revisit some of the points made earlier with regards to overall brain maturation.

If you recall from Chapter Two, the brain is comprised of three prominent regions — the brainstem, limbic system and cerebrum — and long before the higher order thinking regions of the brain fully mature, the brainstem and limbic system are operating with great efficiency. In other words, the brainstem is fairly mature at birth, which helps to ensure that the regulation of blood pressure, heart rate, body temperature and other significant physiological mechanisms are fully functioning. The brainstem also works in tandem with the limbic system to maintain the fight or flight mechanism — a key component of the brain that has ensured human survival over many thousands of years. On its own, key regions of the limbic system, most notably the amygdala and the various limbic structures that govern appetite, sleep, alertness, emotional reactivity, attachment and feelings, mature next. This is then followed by the maturation of the cerebrum and, in particular, the prefrontal cortex. While there is some degree of maturation of this region in the first few years of life there is a great deal of work that occurs through adolescence and into adulthood. In some respects it might be easiest to think of the brain maturing from the inside out and from the back around to the front.

While mapping out a trajectory of brain development seems simple enough, the same cannot be said with regards to the exact systems related to emotional development. In itself, the word 'emotion' is not easily defined and, neurologically speaking, children, as well as adults, are likely to engage a wide array of neural circuitry simultaneously when processing emotional stimuli. Depending on where you look you are also likely to find little consensus on a definition of the term 'emotion' and that the words 'emotions' and 'feelings' are often used synonymously. To simplify things this book relies on definitions found in texts on neuroscience where emotions are often described as the activation of neurological circuits that prioritise our experiences into things we should pay attention to or things we can safely ignore. Feelings, on the other hand, are how we subjectively describe the experiences that emerge from the activations associated with emotion. In other words, our feelings are a product of how our brain processes and attends to emotional stimulation and, consequently, our capacity to mediate our emotions and express different feelings improves as we grow older.

As noted above, the limbic system matures relatively quickly compared to the areas of the brain responsible for higher order thinking. In the earliest years of life children become quite capable of emotional processing and expression, however, during this time they are not as able as their parents or older siblings to moderate the expression of overwhelming feelings and have a limited ability to control their emotions, especially when it comes to focusing or sustaining attention. Prior to their first birthday a child's emotional reactions are instinctual or arguably primitive. From one to three years of age emotional reactions improve but with each successive year a child will demonstrate greater capacity for thinking about emotional situations and working through their emotions accordingly. An individual's ability to moderate frustration, aggression and impulsivity is age-related and, as a function of brain maturation and growth, continually develops and improves over time. As infants, and as yet without the capacity to speak, children smile when pleased or cry when they are hungry, cold, wet or somehow uncomfortable. Those expressions of emotion may then, in turn, be altered through interactions with the people who respond accordingly to those emotional cues. These types of interactions are further evidence that brain development is a product of nature and nurture and this is reinforced as children move through toddlerhood.

As children move from infancy to toddlerhood their emotional development and numerous emotional states can appear far more complex than when they just cried because they were hungry. From one to three years of age children are becoming far more active and independent in the world around them, demonstrating greater language skills, forging new relationships, learning to manage their feelings and connecting with the world in more complex ways. However, while children are increasingly engaging with their world in new and often exciting ways, they still lack the emotional resilience and social skills of their older siblings, caregivers and parents. Much of this may be due to personality but may also be intimately linked with temperament.

Temperament is one of the most fascinating aspects of difference between children and fodder for much comparison between children and/or parenting methods. It is also interesting to note that such discussions even occur within one family by parents who have more than one child and are astounded at how different their children can be when it comes to how each child mediates various emotional stimuli or engages with the world around them. Even in the earliest stages of life children can demonstrate vastly different temperaments. One child may be described as high maintenance compared to the other child who sleeps better, fusses less, cries less and shows greater independence. Some people attribute such things to individual personalities; however, while adults may interchange the terms 'personality' and 'temperament' quite readily, they are in fact quite different.

The word 'personality' conjures up many ideas and definitions and 'temperament' could be considered part of a person's overall personality. A simple definition of temperament, then, would be the characteristic ways people respond to emotional events, novel stimuli and their own impulses and, as such, temperament is often considered an individual emotional characteristic or genetic trait. Temperament is a very important component of a child's emotional capabilities and ability to pay attention and it can impact on a child's motivation, values, social skills and overall behaviour.

Research into child development has a long history when it comes to studying temperament. For many years, psychologists and researchers suggested that biology had little relevance for understanding behavioural variations between children. This has changed significantly over the last couple of decades, and while we still have a great deal to learn about the neural basis of most aspects of behaviour, there is growing agreement in the scientific community that some behavioural and psychological differences among children are attributable to the inheritance of specific biological profiles. To date we know very little about the neurobiological foundations influencing why one child may be more inquisitive than another, more sociable than another, more shy than another, more irritable than another and so on, but science has uncovered important links between temperament, emotional regulation and the prefrontal cortex of the brain.

Richard J Davidson is a neuroscientist and Professor of Psychology and Psychiatry and the Director of the University of Wisconsin's Lab for Affective Neuroscience. In his work Professor Davidson has found that the left side of the prefrontal cortex is very active when it comes to processing positive, extroverted emotions related to setting and attaining goals. Its right-sided counterpart, however, is more active in withdrawal and negative emotions. In other words, Professor Davidson has found that people whose left prefrontal cortex is more active generally tend to be more optimistic and extroverted than those whose right prefrontal cortex is more active and who tend to be pessimistic and withdrawn. Importantly, these differences are also reflected in temperament where related studies found that the behaviour in children who had greater activity in the right frontal cortex was more fearful and shy and, conversely, that children who were more extroverted displayed greater activity in the left frontal cortex. This is also supported by current understandings of the limbic system and, in particular, how the amygdala plays a role in mediating incoming emotional stimuli which can also impact on an individual's temperament. Taken collectively, the research above suggests that neurobiology may play a role in temperament but like many other contemporary understandings of the brain, there is still much to learn regarding the possible innate characteristics of temperament. Much of our understanding of the nature of temperament is still limited in scope and detail. What is clear, however, is that like many of the other aspects of development, the innate characteristics of a child's temperament are also influenced by the environment in which they grow and learn. As a child grows older and continues to engage with the world in various ways, his brain will continue to change and grow as well. In this sense the impact of nurture continues to define the cognitive, emotional, physical and social nature of a child. Each of these areas of development receives greater attention later in this book with regards to how best to nurture such development. The important role of the environment in terms of development also becomes increasingly evident when children reach their fourth birthday and enter more formal learning environments; this too is covered in greater detail in the next chapter and throughout the remainder of this book.

Chapter 5

How the brain gets ready for school

*Most of us believe that in order to learn something we must
work hard at it, and too many have forgotten that the process of
meaningful learning can be fun, exciting and even playful.
Yet the human brain changes during development,
and the 'work', as well as the fun, that is appropriate for teenagers
and adults is not right for young children.*

— Jane M Healey, teacher and educational psychologist

I remember searching through the television channels one day looking for something to occupy my time and coming across one of the many current affairs shows presented in the late afternoon; it immediately caught my attention. In this particular program, an 'expert' in reading was professing that a program he devised could be used to get two-year-olds to read. Wow! Gleeful parents on screen watched in amazement as their young daughter appeared to be reading and I could see the wheels of their minds turning ... reading at two, algorithms by five, early entry into high school and prior to leaving the teenage years studying at Harvard or perhaps Oxford. In my experience and throughout my professional career I have seen many 'experts' attempt to sell programs marketed as pathways to early school success. And while all parents would like to see their children succeed and do well academically, to date there isn't any credible evidence to support the types of programs noted above. Was the girl reading? Perhaps! Or maybe she was recognising the shapes of some words after being marinated in flashcards or inundated with repetition. Was she comprehending what she could derive from print? More importantly, how much time and energy was expended to get her to perform what we would expect older children to do? And what might her young brain have been missing out on while being programmed to read? Learning to read is an important skill but years of experience and more knowledge about the developing brain tell us that pushing young children to do things they are not ready for can create more problems than benefits, regardless of how well they might perform on demand in front of a camera. This is certainly true of four to six-year-olds and the following chapter will provide further insights into the maturing brain for parents in an effort to enhance their understanding of how a child's brain changes as it gets ready to enter and participate in formal 'schooling'.

One of the most fascinating things parents can observe that is demonstrative of a maturing brain is when their children start asking questions that have answers or when children begin annoying their parents with 'why' questions. Why do we have to go to the supermarket? Why do we need to eat? Why do we get sick if we don't eat? Why do you ask me why I ask why all the time? These types of questions gradually emerge about the time that children approach their fourth birthday and move towards entering some measure of formal educational environment, be it kindergarten, preschool or one of the ubiquitous 'early learning' centres that appear in many suburbs or school campuses. As children move out of toddlerhood they become increasingly independent, inquisitive and engaging and they want to know the 'what' and 'why' of just about everything around them. This is due to the fact that their brains are maturing and as they do the skills we looked at in the previous chapter are improving and thus providing greater opportunities for children's social skills to broaden.

When looking at how the brain matures and the related changes in a child's skills and behaviours, it is important to keep in mind that, because of the dynamic nature and overall complexity of each individual child's brain, it is almost impossible to note an exact timetable for such changes for each child. Every brain is unique in many respects and, as a result, there are differences between children in terms of developmental milestones. However, there do appear to be a number of significant changes that occur between a child's fourth and sixth year that, excluding any injuries or impairments, will announce themselves in what all children can say and do.

One of the most interesting things parents will need to keep in mind is that their children will eat more and, indeed, need to eat more. The brain will use about 30 per cent of a child's energy via glucose consumption. The highest levels of glucose consumption and energy use occurs in the prefrontal cortices, suggesting that there is a great deal of growth and maturation taking place in this important region of the brain.

Another important part of a child's brain that is changing is the reticular activating system (RAS). During this time of life the RAS is myelinating extensively and generating greater synaptic connections. The RAS performs many functions but two of the most important are maintaining alertness and consciousness. Parents will begin to see improvements in attention and focus in their children. Concurrently, electrical activity in the brain as measured by electroencephalograms (EEGs — the recording of electrical activity along the scalp) shows improvements in the synchronisation of neural activity or what is referred to as *coherence*. Because of enhanced coherence the brain is better able to integrate the 'past' with the 'present'. Children will show increasingly greater understanding of these concepts and begin to articulate that in their conversations.

Links to the past and present are also apparent and manifest themselves through a child's growing memory capacities. During this stage of life some of the brain's neurons that produce the amino acid acetylcholine appear and at the same time the hippocampus and amygdala are creating greater connections within the limbic system across other regions of the brain. Acetylcholine assists in long-term memory while the hippocampus and amygdala are also part of the brain's memory system and so memories become clearer. Moreover, many early experiences have now been encoded in long-term memory throughout various regions of the brain and hence a number of skills developed early in life become more automatic. This continues to improve with age. As skills become automatic (that is, decoding words and rudimentary writing) the brain is free to focus on content and comprehension. This leads to a greater development and reliance on memory for learning new tasks.

It is also worth noting that beginning around the age of four the emotional part of the brain becomes better connected with the factual/

rational part of the brain (frontal lobes) allowing for improvements in impulse control and self-regulatory behaviour (self-regulation is an important aspect of emotional and social development and is covered in greater detail in Chapter Eight). However, and with regards to the frontal lobes, another important chemical worth mentioning here is the neurotransmitter dopamine. Dopamine plays a role in concentration, attention and motivation, and at this stage in a child's life, levels of dopamine in the region of the frontal lobes known as the prefrontal cortex are nearly at the same levels found in adults. The prefrontal cortex plays an important role in goal-directed behaviour and so children begin to demonstrate increasing capacities and use of this type of behaviour.

While there are changes occurring within the limbic system and prefrontal cortices, other regions of the brain are changing too. Maturation of particular regions within the brain's parietal lobes that are associated with mathematical skills see children being able to count, at times in the right order, and over time with greater accuracy and with increasingly larger numbers. Furthermore, regions of the left temporal lobe are also changing. Increased blood flow in the left hemisphere coincides with dendrite growth in Broca's area. Broca's area and Wernicke's area also show greater connectivity. Broca's area is the brain's grammar and syntax area while Wernicke's area is the comprehension centre. As a child reaches the age of six, greater dendritic patterns and connections are emerging and evident in the right hemisphere as well. Given these important maturational changes in the brain, all aspects of language skills improve: sentences become more grammatically correct, syntax improves and a child's vocabulary increases markedly.

Finally, not unlike the myelination of the RAS noted previously, increases in myelin are evident throughout a number of other regions of the brain including the limbic system, frontal parietal and temporal lobes, cerebellum, and regions of the corpus callosum. An increase in myelin allows for greater connectivity of brain regions and correlates with increased development in various cognitive functions and motor skills. Greater connectivity between the parietal and temporal lobes via the corpus callosum due to myelination facilitates greater comprehension and word-meaning skills. The changes here see improvements in many aspects of language with increasing competence in reading and comprehension, while greater connections in the frontal lobes see a growing capacity to link details to events. Motor skills also show marked improvement as does visual–motor coordination and, as a result, your involvement in tasks such as tying your child's shoelaces starts to diminish. And at the risk of appearing repetitive, emotions gain greater stability and a child begins to regulate emotions while also demonstrating improvements in memory. Memory strategies begin to develop and six-year-olds begin to demonstrate specific strategies for remembering things rather than repeating information over and over again out loud as evident in younger children.

It should now be apparent that a great deal of neurodevelopmental change occurs from ages four to six and with these changes also come enhanced capacities and skills that become increasingly pronounced as children grow older. From four years of age children become increasingly adept at counting, understanding moments in time (that is, days, weeks, time of day, etc.), comparing sets of items, labelling and classifying things in the world around them, asking questions about abstract ideas (that is, death, living things, etc.), differentiating between fantasy and reality and developing problem-solving skills. Not surprisingly, parents can become quite fatigued meeting the needs of these inquisitive minds. And while it is not possible for parents to see their children's brains change and minds evolve, it is possible to watch how that is playing out in terms of many observable characteristics across a broad array of developmental milestones.

Maturing brain, different child

Some of the most obvious developmental changes parents will see in their children are those associated with overall physical growth and improvements in motor-coordination skills. Children are born active but from roughly four years of age they will increasingly engage in long periods of play and physical activity. They are better at walking, running, jumping, hopping and unfortunately, depending on your anxiety levels, climbing. As the brain's myelin increases a child literally moves from being a wobbly two-year-old to a body in constant and increasingly fluid motion. There are also obvious advances in hand–eye coordination, balance, improved manual dexterity, and fine and gross motor coordination. Children become increasingly better at complex movements ranging from learning to copy letters and print, tying shoelaces, getting dressed and undressed and riding a bicycle with training wheels.

One of the biggest joys parents can see with their children's increased mobility and coordination is the enthusiasm and satisfaction their children show even though they are far from mastering many motor skills. It is therefore important to support a child's desire for activity and play, for we also know that children's skill levels during this period of development will vary based on their amount of physical activity — more activity means more opportunities to improve coordination and motor skills. It is also important to note that there is a large body of research telling us that across a range of developmental domains, sedentary children fall behind children who participate in activities like sports, dance lessons and outdoor play. In other words science is demonstrating links between all aspects of development and that exercise and movement are not just important for the body but also for the brain.

Aside from changes in physical growth and enhanced motor skills, another obvious indicator of a maturing mind is a child's communication skills. Language capacities expand rapidly at four years of age and most parents would generally attest to the fact that their four-year-old has a larger vocabulary and talks more with greater proficiency than a three-year-old. At four, children communicate in sentences that are increasingly complex, have fewer pronunciation errors and demonstrate a growing vocabulary. It is important to point out that these improvements in oral language occur naturally and without formal instruction. As a child matures so too do neural connections in the brain related to language and memory while myelination throughout both hemispheres allows for enhanced communication and by extension greater opportunities to learn many new things. For young children, learning is improved through asking questions and by the time they are able to speak in fuller sentences, children will also ask increasingly complex questions, often beginning with 'why'.

As children move closer to their sixth birthday their conversational skills expand rapidly. Well-developed language skills are evident through clearer pronunciation; expanded, complex and grammatically correct sentences; and a substantive vocabulary. Children at this age also begin to incorporate greater details in their conversations, show a developing understanding of the pragmatics of language and demonstrate that they can wait for their turn to speak. Moreover, a child's improved language also helps in other aspects of the transition from toddlerhood to childhood through marked improvement in emotional control and a greater understanding of how to engage in social environments in a positive manner.

Oral language skills, like the physical skills noted above, are fairly obvious indicators that a child is maturing or 'growing up'. It is, however, important to note that somewhere around their fourth birthday children will also become better at managing intense emotions and learn what causes certain feelings. They also begin to understand the feelings of others and social interactions with peers begin to flourish. By the time they are ready to enter a formal school environment, and excluding any developmental problems or unforeseen psychological difficulties, most children will continue to demonstrate improved impulse control and become more independent at managing their feelings. These new skills will allow children to better manage themselves in social situations and help them form and maintain friendships with other children and adults. Friendships and acceptance into various social groups become increasingly important, as does a child's growing ability to mediate emotions and demonstrate a greater awareness of the emotions of others. Many studies show that children who do not develop a minimal level of social competence by the age of six are not only at risk of a range of individual social inadequacies and difficulties related to developing relationships in later life, but are also more likely to drop out of school before completing Year Twelve. It is equally significant to mention that, not unlike when they were infants, six-year-olds still draw a great deal of emotional stability though their secure and loving relationships with others. Once again the message that safety and security ensure healthy emotional development is apparent, but safe and secure relationships are also integral for the continued development of cognitive capacities.

As noted above, improvements in your child's memory, concentration levels and attention result from increased neural connectivity and the maturation of structures and processes in the brain. Improved connectivity in the maturing brain also sees the brain performing with greater efficiency and with every measure currently available to science we know that children's brains perform faster as they get older — faster performance means enhanced cognitive capacities, better overall neural efficiency and increased intellectual growth. The types of skills and capacities associated with learning and brain maturation receive greater attention in the next chapter but it is important to understand that with brain maturation comes greater independence and as children become increasingly independent and self-reliant, they demonstrate greater curiosity and a willingness to try new experiences, often at the expense of parents who fret about their children hurting themselves.

Finally, and by the time they are ready to enter school, children will have longer attention spans, engage in robust conversations and decision-making processes and ask questions that are more analytical. For some, this rapid time of neural growth characterised by a range of improvements across a number of developmental domains has become a platform for greater (that is, more) 'educational' endeavour under the mantra of 'enrichment'. However, in terms of healthy brain development, doing 'more' with or to children may actually result in achieving less.

Education is not a race!

Throughout the first few chapters of this book the links between experience and the developing brain have been discussed along with insights into how various experiences help to shape a person's neurological architecture. Perhaps this is one of the most important findings in recent neuroscientific research: experiences influence the brain and, by association, behaviour and learning. Historically many educators and parents have known that experience plays a part in learning, albeit from a more intuitive perspective given that we have only recently been able to look at a brain in action. As alluded to earlier, one of the negative consequences of advances in our collective understanding of the brain has seen the growth of some rather deceptively attractive links made between experiences, neural stimulation in relation to enrichment and academic achievement. In order to understand this more fully, a quick review of the important points from Chapter Two is required.

If you recall, neurons provide the raw material for learning by building connections in the brain. This process begins about seventeen days after conception. In these early stages of life neurons also become differentiated to assume specialised roles and form connections with other neurons, enabling them to communicate and store information. We also know that the brain expects, and depends on, particular types of stimulation which, in turn, activate certain connections and that repetition consolidates these connections and the brain learns.

In themselves the types of experiences that impact on neural development are also greatly influenced by a neurodevelopmental timetable that extends from birth through childhood and into adulthood. This timetable is, in turn, influenced by the production of myelin, the white fatty material that insulates the axons of neurons. Myelin aids in the transmission of information from one neuron to another and the more 'myelinated' axons in the brain, the greater the opportunity for neural information to be passed more efficiently and quickly. What this means is that it is much easier to learn and do particular things when regions of the brain are sufficiently myelinated. It is also important for parents to remember that a great deal of myelin production occurs well into the teens and does not completely finish until their children are in their twenties (at the time of writing, the available research suggests that complete myelination finishes in females sometime before the age of 25, while males might take a few years longer). In other words, the build-up and acquisition of myelin towards full brain maturation is more marathon than sprint and learning really is something that is 'lifelong'.

At this point you may asking yourself what does myelination have to do with school? Well, some scientists believe that periods of myelination could be referred to as 'learning windows' and these windows represent prime times for learning. There are also three important points related to myelination that are useful to remember: different regions of the brain myelinate at different times; a healthy brain knows which areas need to be myelinated first; and myelination in all regions of the brain does not happen all at once. Taken in totality this means that there are developmentally optimum times to engage with particular types of learning and there isn't any evidence to suggest that this can be hurried along through enrichment, more instruction or extra tuition. It is also important to note that while 'learning windows' represent the optimum time for particular types of stimulation and learning, the windows never actually close completely and there do not appear to be any capacities that are completely lost as we get older. As adults we can always learn new things but as children some of those things come much more easily. For example, the learning windows for language and instrumental music are open widest from roughly birth to eleven years of age and three to eleven years of age, respectively. Children can and will learn more than one language in bilingual or trilingual environments, or learn to play the piano with the appropriate stimulation, but the same measure of instruction comes much easier to a four-year-old than to mum or dad.

A further important consideration related to myelination and education is that while the idea of 'learning windows' presents interesting opportunities to engage in broad discussions of how this research might contribute to formal educational endeavour, they may also be responsible for more worrisome educational trends. Given that experiences play a role in neural development and that a young brain is maturing rapidly, there are some who believe that the earlier and more plentiful the stimulation the better it might be for a child's overall educational future. This has led to misguided notions of what might constitute enhanced neural stimulation and a burgeoning industry marketing educational toys, games and paraphernalia to parents of babies, toddlers and children.

The previous chapter noted how ideas surrounding notions of 'enrichment' might be misconstrued or used inappropriately when it comes to young children. As children grow closer to school age, enrichment opportunities marketed in different ways and with a view to giving children a competitive edge at school success have given rise to an alarmingly increasing trend of extra tuition and extra curricular activity for children at younger and younger ages. This has been exacerbated by a parallel growth in a wide range of educational products for enhancing 'early learning' and building cognitive capacities. Quite often the science behind such propositions is very faulty or has been used incorrectly, resulting in the emergence of a number of interesting myths related to the brain and learning. For example, there isn't any evidence to support the notion that playing Mozart to an unborn child will improve his or her math scores or that listening to classical music will make children smarter. There also isn't any truth to commercials, programs or packaging stating that exposing infants or toddlers to language DVDs will boost their vocabulary or that the fundamental functions of the left and right hemisphere of a child's brain can be enhanced through proper training. In all, much of the hype using neuroscience to support unsubstantiated claims for building academic prowess in children is, at best, erroneous and, at worst, completely misleading. Therefore, to help bring this chapter to a close, it is useful to further clarify and reiterate some significant points related to experience, neural connectivity and learning.

First of all, while we know that input from the environment helps to shape the brain and that experiences are important, it is important to also remember that there are differences among children and trying to advance developmental timelines with the use of 'enrichment' tools or programs can do more harm than good. Consider trying to get young children to write before the fine motor skills and manual dexterity required to hold a pencil are neurologically established in the brain. If your child is introduced to a writing instrument designed for an adult and asked to engage in formal penmanship too early they may develop an 'incorrect' pencil grip. This, in turn, becomes neurologically hardwired to the extent that trying to correct that grip later in school becomes very difficult, if not impossible, and is often coupled with a great deal of stress. In a sense a child's brain is being asked to 'unlearn' a particular way of holding a pencil because a 'learning window' may have been forced open too early. Consider that if something as relatively mundane as a pencil grip can be hampered by trying to do too much too soon, what might happen to children when they are placed in situations and asked to engage in other types of activities beyond the developmental timetable of their brain. Our current understanding of the brain and, in particular, the mechanisms of neural proliferation, is still in its infancy. However, it is widely recognised that learning windows have a very wide gap of opportunity for their development and there isn't any evidence to suggest that getting children to do things sooner is better. In fact, there are reasons to suspect the contrary given that there exists a number of other contributing factors that combine to influence neural proliferation and connectivity, including genetic makeup, environment, the sum of experiences we have imposed on our brains and the activity we are bombarding it with now and into the future. In other words while stimulation is important for learning, so too is a child's developmental timeline and social context.

Second, and equally important when looking at any notion of enhanced skill acquisition or learning, is the realisation that it is not possible to accelerate emotional maturation since regions of the limbic system have their own time clock. Trying to have children do too much too soon by performing certain tasks or producing certain results may also engulf children in undue stress beyond their limited coping abilities. In fact, for some children, too much too soon can lead to stress-related anxieties that actually turn off thinking processes and do more harm than good. Misguided beliefs surrounding a 'more is better approach' under the guise of enrichment without informed understanding of overall child development or how the brain grows and matures can contribute to a range of emotional problems or may even hinder development in other important regions of the brain. One of the world's leading authorities in neuroscience and paediatric medicine, Professor Peter Huttenlocher of the University of Chicago's School of Medicine, has suggested that overly ambitious agendas related to enrichment and teaching programs for children may lead to what can be referred to as 'neurological crowding' whereby attempts at overstimulation can lead to crowding effects and to early decreases in the size and number of brain regions in children that are largely unspecified and that may be necessary for creativity in adolescence and adulthood. Professor Huttenlocher has also argued that 'new' enrichment programs should be carefully scrutinised given that studies of the effects of 'neurological crowding' suggest that too much early learning can prove detrimental to later learning, or as noted earlier, more may end up being less.

Finally, and in the context of enrichment, schooling and learning, it is important to reiterate that the term 'enrichment' remains somewhat of an elusive construct. This is especially true when 'enrichment' is linked to acceleration or somehow improving the development of children who are relatively on track for normal healthy development. To that end, questions and ideas about ensuring that a child's unplanned and planned learning experiences are timely and sufficient at the intersection of normal brain development become important considerations for parents. The second half of this book sets out to provide insights into these important areas. This begins with the following chapter, which looks at contemporary notions of 'learning' and neurological development and is followed by chapters on language development, social and emotional development, intelligence and education.

Chapter 6

Learning and the brain

Children enter the world with an inborn growth schedule that is the product of several million years of biological evolution. They are pre-eminently wise about what they need and what they are ready and not ready to do.

— William Crain, psychologist

I love listening to parents chat when they are picking up their children from school. I'm not one to eavesdrop but listening to parents is compelling, given my line of work, for it is not uncommon to hear parents discuss their child's achievements, especially when it comes time to compare report cards. I am often entertained and puzzled at the same time. Entertained by the opportunities to brag and puzzled by adult notions of learning and success at school. Don't get me wrong, I often find myself speaking of my own children's achievements with gusto, and while I would never admit to living vicariously through my kids, I am hopeful my son will play soccer for Barcelona as planned. That being said, I am also mindful that any successes my children have will also be tempered by failures and disappointment and that learning is, indeed, a lifelong process marked by a variety of indicators of success. In this chapter I offer some of the latest ideas surrounding new understandings of learning while at the same time briefly discussing some outdated views on schooling and achievement.

Defining 'learning'

What is learning? This seems like an obviously simplistic question. However, dig a bit deeper into the word and it is not necessarily easy to define. Is it the product of some type of activity or is it a process of some sort? The origin of the word 'learn' dates from Old English meaning 'to get knowledge' or to 'be cultivated' and dictionary definitions of learning often focus on the acquisition of knowledge through study. Thus it would seem that learning is both a product and a process.

As a subject of research, learning has generated many different theories related to how people learn. Universities house many volumes of books regarding the topic and there are more than 50 different theories about how people learn. Given the large amount of literature and research on learning it is beyond the scope of this book to outline all the theories and theorists … to be honest, it would probably not be all that helpful for parents anyway. Instead, this chapter explores learning with a few important points in mind. First, and as noted above, learning is both a product and a process. Second, learning is also about *making sense* of the world and *interpreting and understanding reality* in different ways. Third, learning does not just happen in schools and is not as easily measured as some might suggest. Fourth, discussions of learning in this chapter focus on its neurological and cognitive aspects and not the acquisition of emotional and social capacities or the impact of those capacities on learning. That will be part of the discussion in later chapters but it needs to be said that from a neurological perspective whenever a person is in the process of learning via sensory stimulation this not only induces a physical/ cognitive reaction but also an emotional one. Add any number of people to any learning experience and there is also a degree of social influence. Therefore, 'learning' can never be isolated as either a cognitive, physical, emotional or social endeavour but rather is the product of some or all of the above. For simplicity's sake, this chapter targets cognition or what most people would generally describe as the process of acquiring information. Finally, and most importantly, all children can and do learn every day and this powerful human characteristic begins long before children enter school and continues long after they graduate.

As noted in earlier chapters, learning starts sooner than we might think. For neuroscientists, learning is a neurobiological process that begins about three weeks after conception. It is at this time of human development that the neural tube in the brain closes and neurons emerge, move to different regions in the brain and start talking to one another. If you can recall from Chapter Two, neurons 'talk' to each other as the brain responds to environmental stimuli and this 'talking' helps to build the neural connections of the brain. Therefore, learning occurs via environmental stimuli, and once a child leaves the womb, learning increases at a phenomenal rate and is further developed through the complex interactions a child has with other people. Importantly, the building of neural connections and a child's ability to learn is also linked to the growth of myelin (the white fatty material that coats the axons of a neuron) and the more myelin a person has, the better neurons can communicate and ultimately hardwire for certain abilities.

At birth, a child will have very few myelinated axons. This is one reason why newborns have such poor eyesight and limited physical abilities; the neural networks necessary for vision and movement aren't well established and working fast enough. It should therefore be apparent that the growth of myelin, or 'myelination', is incredibly important and, in the end, the neurobiological processes underpinning learning are determined by myelination and nothing can be done to hasten this process.

Learning is also about experiencing the world, storing information, engaging with others and is a continual process of renewal and revision. It is always a joy to watch children, as this is when you often see learning in its purest sense. When children are in the midst of safe and supportive environments they self-direct their learning by engaging and responding to the world around them and as they grow and mature so too does their brain and this capacity to learn. In spite of all the research that is now available, many people are simply not aware of how the brain grows or they forget that the brain takes time to mature because they can't actually see a brain change in the same way they notice that they are constantly buying sneakers to accommodate growing feet. However, while we cannot physically watch a brain grow, the research tells us some very important things related to children and learning.

One of the most important considerations related to learning is that, while it is not uncommon to associate learning with remembering, there are subtle differences between learning and memory and major differences between the memory capacities of an adult and those of a child. Moreover, and not unlike the numerous and diverse range of theories about learning, our understanding of memory and how memory actually works in the human brain is also varied, widely studied and to date not yet well understood.

Studies of memory date back at least 100 years and there are whole research departments attached to universities that are looking to acquire a better understanding of something we all take for granted; that is, until we grow older and our memory is less reliable. Interestingly, the number of studies related to the neurological foundations of memory have probably only been surpassed by the number of researchers saying that we know so very little about how we remember things, why some people are better than others at remembering and why memory seems to be less reliable as we grow older. Nobel Laureate and perhaps the world's leading authority on memory, Professor Eric Kandel, believes that memory represents a large family of deep problems and that we are only beginning to understand how memory works within the human mind. Nonetheless, we do know that we have different types of memories, that memory is a result of thinking and/or doing, that the brain stores memories in different ways, and that certain types of memories are not very reliable.

One of the many illusions we tend to have about memory is that we often think of it in the same way we think of video recordings. During the day-to-day events of our lives we store much of what we do in the brain and then call upon those events and their details when we need to remember them. However, unlike a video recorder, memories are not stored in one place but are broken up and moved throughout different regions of the brain. When trying to remember something, the brain relies on the billions of connections throughout many structures to pull our memories together.

For example, the first time a child sees and tastes a lemon, the shape, colour, smell and taste are categorised and stored in different parts of the brain. From that point forward, every experience of a lemon results in a composite memory of 'lemon' from simultaneous recollections from each of those regions which, in turn, helps to reinforce the existing memory. We don't think about this process consciously and the memory of a lemon is a highly complex neurological process that we often take for granted because it happens so naturally. As natural as it may seem, however, not all types of memories are the same and how we receive, encode and store information varies.

In every moment of every day our senses are busy taking in thousands of bits of information. Much of this information is filtered away from our conscious attention. If this wasn't the case we would literally lose our mind in a vast sea of neural activity. However, on some occasions we need to attend to information that is presented to us and we store this information in different parts of the brain and hold it for fractions of a second. This is referred to as 'immediate memory' and it is very unreliable and often frustrating. For example, if at this moment you decided to order something for dinner from your favourite takeaway restaurant, you might experience immediate memory first-hand. This happens when you find the phone number in the *Yellow Pages*, put down the directory, and make the call. If your call is answered and your order is placed then all is well and you move on to other activities until you go to get your food. If, however, the line is busy and you need to redial later, you will, in all likelihood, need to look for the number again as your brain is unlikely to keep that information at hand. That is the essence of immediate memory and most memory scientists believe that it lasts about 30 seconds depending on the importance or significance of the information. That is why emergency numbers are short and catchy — call 000 — while other important numbers, such as that of the local police station, are entered into the speed dials of our phones.

An extended version of immediate memory is 'short-term memory', or 'working memory', and this is part of the executive function of the prefrontal cortices. The prefrontal cortices receive information, keep it available for immediate use and coordinate its use by other parts of the brain. If your son or daughter were to interrupt you right at this very moment and ask what you were doing, you would use your short-term memory to tell them you are reading about memory. Working memory allows us to carry out the many tasks we do each day and also ensures that we do not overload our brain by allowing it to easily forget unimportant or insignificant events. Moreover, to better understand the mental workings of children, there are three important aspects of working memory you should, pardon the pun, remember.

First, the simple holding of information in working memory is hard work and attention-demanding, but does improve with age. Before a child's fourth birthday, working memory is limited and unreliable. From four to eight years of age it improves markedly and then shows a more gradual improvement as children move into adolescence where memory performance soon begins to resemble that of an adult. Think about this the next time you give your child a verbal 'to do' list before they can go outside and play; by the time you have told Johnny the fourth thing on the list, he has likely forgotten the first three.

Second, working memory is temporary and wanes quickly. In

terms of formal education this is an important consideration when working with children for it suggests that effective learning activities require constant shifts in duration and style. Having young children sit at desks for too long often results in undesirable behaviour rather than learning. This is explored in greater detail in Chapter Ten.

Finally, some of the latest research on working memory has identified significant links between it and many other important abilities, such as following instructions, coherent thinking, paying attention, note-taking, writing, reasoning, social interactions and complex learning. In this sense it is not uncommon for a child with working-memory problems to experience a range of associated difficulties and potentially struggle in school. Moreover, problems with working memory and any associated learning difficulties may be evident through behavioural problems. And while it is beyond most parents, teachers and schools to diagnose potential neurological difficulties, it is important to remember all children can learn but they may need extra help or some measure of outside assistance or consultation when school activities are overly frustrating or stressful.

Aside from immediate and working memory, the brain can also store memories over a very long time and in many instances over a lifetime. 'Long-term memory' is a vital tool for human beings and often is what most people think of when thinking about memory. Long-term memory is a bit like the hard drive of your computer: information is stored in the brain when the save button is pushed. Unlike a computer, however, long-term memories may be distributed in various regions of the brain and the save button for people lies in the limbic system. The limbic system, or emotional part of the brain, is like a relay station for memory processing. The more that an event causes an emotional response in the brain the more likely it is to be transferred into long-term memory for future recollection. Moreover, pushing the save button results in long-term memories being subdivided into two categories: 'implicit' and 'explicit' memories.

If at this very moment you decided to put this book down and pour a nice glass of wine you would be relying on the implicit memories laid down in your subconscious for the mechanics of pouring and then drinking. If, however, while you were pouring your drink you tried to recall the last time you visited a vineyard, you would be drawing upon your explicit memories. In other words, implicit memory is responsible for embedding a vast array of skills and habits which are often engaged on a subconscious level, while explicit memory encodes factual knowledge. The activities of eating, walking and riding a bike are implicit memories while names, faces, events and dates are types of explicit memories. Although it may appear simple, the retrieval of long-term memories involves complicated neurological processes and the complexity is evident in that implicit memories maintain *procedural* memories while *semantic* and *episodic* memories are found in explicit memories. Each of these relies on different neural structures and connections in the brain.

Procedural memories are those memories of the steps or *procedures* for doing something, they are the 'how' of doing something. Procedural memories become automatic with practice and include such things as handwriting, riding a bike, driving a car, swinging a tennis racquet and tying one's shoes. Episodic memories are the memories of life experiences (episodes) and involve the capacity to place facts and events in time and refer to them freely. It is significant to restate the important role the limbic system plays for ensuring the encoding of long-term memories and in particular, episodic memories. When an event invokes a strong emotional response a person is more likely to remember many, but not all, aspects of the event and what they were doing at the time. For example, those who saw the World Trade Center towers collapse in real time on September 11 have vivid recollections of where they were and what they were doing.

Semantic memories are significantly different from episodic memories in that they are those memories about information and knowledge of the world around us. We use our semantic memory to remember important dates and retain facts and vital pieces of information. Semantic memories are generally devoid of any emotional content and are removed from a specific moment and place (context). When children are given major tests in school it is their semantic memory that they are relying on. Interestingly, if a child has bad memories (episodic memories) of past exam experiences, this can have a negative effect on their exam performance when they attempt to recall information (semantic memory). Therefore, while different memories carry different labels they can impact on one another which further identifies that the brain is a complex web of interconnectivity and that 'schooling' would do well to consider such important ideas in its systems and structures. Further important aspects of memory in relation to 'schooling' are explored in Chapter Nine, but some final considerations related to the reliability and effort required for long-term memory are noted below.

In what month and year did Neil Armstrong walk on the Moon and if you were alive at the time what were you doing when this happened? For those who were alive during the *Apollo* missions, many would struggle to recall that Neil Armstrong stepped on the surface of the Moon on 20 July 1969 but they will have vivid memories of where they were and what they were doing. This is an intriguing paradox due in part to the nature of semantic and episodic memories. Because semantic memories generally focus on facts and verifiable information they are rarely incorrect, unless the information presented was incorrect, but they are exceedingly difficult to draw upon. This is especially true when there is a large gap between information acquisition and information recall. Episodic memories, on the other hand, are easily recalled given their emotional value yet they are seldom accurate and often distorted. Memories, in particular episodic memories, are not exact copies of reality but a recreation of it and, as such, people will inadvertently integrate the details of what they remember with their *expectations* of what they should remember. Our brains do not store all of the information they receive but instead take in particular stimuli and associate this with what we already know and these *fragmented* associations act as cues when we consciously try to remember something. This is why two people can have very different recollections of an event they experienced together and why eye-witness testimony in criminal trials is often fodder for extensive cross examination.

Memory distortions are common for all people but children are more prone to problems of recall due to the immature nature of their developing brain. Indeed, most people have very little, if any, memories of experiences before the age of three or four and some researchers believe this is due to the immature nature of a child's brain and their lack of experiences to tie events together, which occurs as we grow older. Fortunately, as children grow and mature so too does their capacity to remember and learn and, as noted earlier, this is intimately linked with how they experience the world around them.

From the beginning of this chapter we have looked at learning as part of a neurobiological process requiring sensory input from the environment. While it may seem repetitive, there are a number of reasons why this cannot be emphasised enough. First, the developing brain requires a variety of sensory, perceptual and motor experiences and learning is a product of these experiences. All of the experiences necessary for optimum development are usually easy to meet unless a child is born with a visual, auditory or motor deficit or lives in a problematic environment. Moreover, the most important components for ensuring healthy growth, development and learning are not pre-packaged educational programs or toys. For children, healthy neural development and learning is derived from nurturing, stable and consistent relationships. Natural abilities in the brain appear in the early years of life when parents and caregivers provide a safe and supportive environment where talking, reading, responding to nonverbal cues and playing are the norm and not the exception. Overall, the best stimulation and enrichment is derived from loving interactions with people who provide rich opportunities to explore and discover the world, and this is critical during the first five years of life.

Second, from infancy to toddlerhood to the first days of school, children are engaged in intense intellectual development much of which was not well understood as recently as 30 or so years ago. Contemporary research tells us that infants do have some form of immature memories and engage in numerical reasoning, while older children make sense of the world on many different levels. We also know that children affect their interactions and environments at the same time as their interactions and environments are affecting them.

For example, when an infant smiles or grimaces they receive some measure of feedback from the adults around them which, in turn, may form memories to be used later and/or elicit some behavioural response. Furthermore, aside from the adverse impact of exposure to some forms of trauma, no single thing is more important than any other in that the first few years of life are comprised of a collection of experiences that will impact on early cognitive development and learning.

Third, while there is a growing industry suggesting that specialised learning programs and early exposure to academic tutelage or educational 'enrichment' programs can accelerate learning, such claims lack substantive research evidence. Yes, it is true that the brain is the most malleable in the first few years of life and stimulation is important, but learning occurs over a lifetime and children should not be prepped for college when they are just learning to speak or walk. Remember that the brain's developmental timelines are based on a complex interplay of nature and nurture and stretch over a number of years. Simply trying to 'educate' a child as soon as possible with a view to enhancing later academic achievement perpetuates misguided information and naive understandings of child development, and learning becomes rife with difficulties. In the Information Age, notions of enhancing learning via various forms of media have exacerbated this and created a great deal of unsubstantiated hype and potential long-term problems.

The brain does not mature in a nice, neat linear fashion and while it is very malleable and eager for stimulation at an early age it is not mature enough to deal with rampant technological wizardry or hyper-educational instruction. Simply stated, there is little, if any, evidence to suggest that a child's intellect, learning capacities or overall neural development can be enhanced via electronic games or computer products, which are often marketed as tools for improving early learning and/or academic success. Indeed, what these products may actually be doing is diminishing cognitive performance for they require children to be sedentary and primarily passive recipients of information. Albert Einstein was a baby at one point in time but 'Baby Einstein' is unlikely to enhance learning let alone build a new genius. Instead, children need to be active and require the provision of stimuli in the form of toys or a play area which is more than enough for a child given that the human brain is an innately curious mechanism and an insatiable problem solver. The real physical world of natural sensory stimulation is where a child's brain needs to interact. Again, watch children engage with the world around them and you will see learning at its best.

Chapter 7

How the brain learns to talk

Language learning is a deep puzzle that our theories and machines struggle to solve but children accomplish with ease. How do infants discover the sounds and words used in their particular language(s) when the most sophisticated computers cannot? What is it about the human mind that allows a young child, merely one year old, to understand the words that induce meaning in our collective minds, and to begin to use those words to convey their innermost thoughts and desires?
A child's budding ability to express a thought through words is a breathtaking feat of the human mind.

— Patricia Kuhl, neuroscientist and professor of early childhood learning

For many researchers of child development one of the most fascinating aspects of development is how, without any instruction, children learn to talk. As adults we often take our capacity to communicate for granted, and few of us rarely consider how we learned to speak in the first place. Talking is part of who we are and we do it well, although some do it more than others even when they should not. The acquisition of language and speech remains a mystery to many scientists and to date we continue to learn a great deal about how children go from babbling to 'Mama' to complex sentences with deceptive ease and simplicity. The following chapter sheds some light on what is known about language development in the brain and how this important skill is nurtured from infancy to the first days of school. This chapter is not about the aspects of literacy, which include the particular skill sets of grammar and spelling that need to be taught by early childhood teachers. It is, however, important to clarify the difference between language and literacy in order to avoid the incorrect practice of using the two words interchangeably.

Language is our basic vehicle for communication and a fundamental means of social interaction. Although some have tried to teach language to other species, particularly primates, language — in particular spoken language — is a uniquely human trait. Language allows us to convey many types of information from one person to another and we share our thoughts, emotions and needs with others while using language to pass on aspects of culture from one generation to the next. Our first experience of language develops as an oral skill, which is the principal focus of this chapter, however, over time language is also transmitted through written, symbolic and pictorial forms.

Literacy, on the other hand, refers to a person's capacity to engage with the types of symbols, pictures and signs used to represent language as noted above. Literacy, quite simply, refers to our ability to read and write, and while our capacity for using oral language has been around for millennia, our ability to represent the sounds of language with written symbols is a relatively recent phenomenon. Prior to the beginning of the twentieth century, the vast majority of people on Earth were unable to read and write. Today, however, literacy skills are a general expectation of most societies and feature prominently on agendas for enhancing a person's quality of life. It is now widely recognised that literacy is the fundamental key to educational achievement and a better standard of living, but while the links between literacy and future success and life chances are important, this chapter focuses on how language emerges in the developing brain and contributes to the later development of literacy.

Arguably, the most amazing aspect about a child's development of oral language is that, barring any developmental problems, the vast majority of children learn language and to speak without any major difficulties and without any formal training. Perhaps the only thing as amazing as our capacity for learning to communicate is the sheer volume of research and theories looking at how this happens! In the last couple of decades, our understanding of language development in the brain has grown immensely but it is important to note that we are still in the very early stages of unlocking the neural mechanisms underlying language development. What we do know is that some aspects of language development appear universal and are complemented by our understanding of the brain.

One of the most interesting things about language development is that children in all cultures learn to speak in a remarkably regular way and by the ages of four or five can speak in full and complex sentences. In order to do this all children will learn, without much difficulty, some important rules of language, whether they are attempting to speak English, French, Mandarin or Swahili. In what appears to be a fairly linear format, children will acquire skills in phonology, morphology, syntax or grammar and then semantics. Without getting too involved in linguistic rules, phonology refers to making meaningful basic sounds such as the vowel and/or consonant sounds (phonemes) found in English. Morphology is the next step and includes the systematic grouping of phonemes into meaningful words or parts of words. From there children begin to learn to incorporate words into sentences. Initial sentences are often fragmented but over time syntax (the rules of combining words into phrases and sentences) will improve and semantics (the meaning of what is intended) becomes clearer.

Oral language is mastered very early in childhood. On their second birthday, most children are well on their way to speaking and by the time they reach six years of age their conversations are not much different to those of any teenage siblings that may be around. It probably goes without saying that the *topics* of conversation for a six- and a thirteen-year-old will be quite different. Moreover, and at the risk of appearing repetitive, prior to their fifth birthday, children across all cultures learn language in a remarkably similar way. The simple sounds an infant makes will turn into babbling which evolves into single words, then two-word phrases and eventually into increasingly complex sentences. The relative ease with which children learn to speak so early stands in stark contrast to the difficulty grown adults face when learning to speak French for their trip to Paris and consequently many theorists believe that language, in itself, may be an innate aspect of a young brain. One such theorist, considered by many to be perhaps the world's leading authority on linguistics, is Professor Noam Chomsky.

Born in 1928, Noam Chomsky continues to write prolifically and is an Emeritus Professor of Linguistics and Philosophy at the prestigious Massachusetts Institute of Technology. In 1957, Chomsky significantly altered our collective understanding of language when he presented a revolutionary theory of language development to the world and coined the phrase 'universal grammar'. In essence, Chomsky suggested that language must be an inherent and innate capacity of the human brain given its universal nature and the fact that all natural languages are similar in how they are structured and function and in the rules that govern them. Chomsky continues to research and write in this area and suggests that the brain's mental grammar allows it to combine verbs, nouns and objects into an endless variety of sentence combinations and that an innate mechanism built into the brain allows children to acquire complex language skills early in life and without direct instruction. Current understandings of the brain appear to support these ideas.

Perhaps the most obvious evidence that language may be part of an innate and distinct component of the brain is how it is localised in particular regions of the brain. Before researchers could look at a human brain in action using modern technology, studies of individuals who had suffered some measure of brain injury or trauma found that the left hemisphere of the brain was responsible for important functions of language. For example, the left hemisphere appears to have a region responsible for comprehension and one responsible for grammar and syntax. If you suffer a stroke in either of these regions you will likely incur some degree of language impairment. However, the right hemisphere of the brain is responsible for prosody or the inflection and musical quality that lends emphasis to verbal communication and affords us with opportunities to add emotional value to what we say and in how we say it. The language regions of the hemispheres are apparent long before we are able to string words into sentences and one interesting study in particular demonstrated this by looking at how babies babbled.

In 2002, a landmark study published in the prestigious journal *Science* found that as early as five months of age babies were demonstrating the use of the left hemisphere for language and the right hemisphere for expressing emotion. The researchers in this study had identified that babies babbled out of the right side of their mouth and when they smiled they used the left side of the mouth. If you recall from previous discussions, the human brain is rather unique in that the left hemisphere controls the right side of the body while the right hemisphere controls the left. To that end, if babies babble out of the right side of the mouth then babbling, which is an early form of oral communication, is being activated and is functioning in the left hemisphere. If you were to videotape adults speaking and watch this in very slow motion you would even find that adults favour the right side of the mouth when speaking. The babbling and smiling study has been supplemented and supported by many other studies and it is now widely accepted that the left hemisphere of the brain is the dominant location for language, that this is evident early in life and that children arrive in the world with an innate predisposition to learn language. For parents then, a key question might be what can be done to ensure that this natural inclination for oral language is helped along in order for 'normal' development to occur?

One of the first things to remember before embarking on a discussion of how to help your child's language skills is that the timetable for learning oral language appears similar for all children. Children in Boston, Barcelona and Brussels will have remarkably similar timelines for learning to speak their respective languages and this timetable starts long before an infant babbles. There is now very strong evidence that learning the sounds of a language begins in the womb and that before they are born babies are eavesdropping on their mother's conversations. One of the ways researchers have discovered this amazing feat has been through monitoring foetal heart rates. It turns out that a baby's heart rate will change quite dramatically at the sound of its mother's voice and complementary studies have identified that newborns prefer their own mother's voice and their own native language and that this is evident as little as two days after leaving the womb. It also appears that a mother's voice is an important stimulus throughout a child's early development and that other forms of stimulation assist in language development.

Information presented in earlier chapters noted the importance of sensory stimulation and that the growth of the neural architecture of the brain occurs before birth. Combine this with the information above and it should not be surprising that children enter the world paying close attention to language, geared to learn and able to understand language at a very young age. Long before they can speak, children are working out words and sentences by detecting sounds and language patterns, by carving language into smaller bits and pieces, without any teaching from their parents or an educational DVD. That being said, there are some important things that assist in the development of language.

From the outset, the most important factor regarding language development is remembering that language is fundamentally a social act. Language does not develop in a vacuum and from birth the daily interactions a child has with people will assist in shaping its language skills. These interactions have such a profound impact early in life that exposure to a particular language in the first year alters the brain to the extent that not long after birth hardwiring for language creates accents and an inability to hear non-native sounds. Somewhere between six and twelve months of age babies start to filter out speech sounds not used in their immediate environment resulting in a loss of sensitivity to speech sounds of foreign languages. Babies are very clever: they pay attention and tune into the sounds around them and will stop attending to unfamiliar sounds or those sounds that are not needed for mastering their own language. This is one of the reasons why native Japanese speakers struggle greatly with differentiating between the sounds made by the English letters 'R' and 'L'. A sign that was proudly hung across one of the most prominent streets in downtown Tokyo not long after World War II in support of Douglas MacArthur's presidential aspirations is testimony to the above: 'We Pray For MacArthur's Erection'! The importance of hearing the sounds of a language in the first year of life through social interactions and for normal development to occur is also evident in extreme cases of neglect or abuse. One of the most tragic cases in history related to abuse and the deprivation of language stimulation is that of 'Genie'.

In November 1970 the case of Genie, a pseudonym given to her by her carers, came to public attention. Genie walked into a social welfare office with her elderly grandmother and nearly blind mother and immediately social workers noticed things were not right with her. She displayed some unusual mannerisms and was so tiny that the social workers believed that she was six or seven years of age. At first, the caseworker attending to Genie thought that she was autistic, given her unusual behaviour and what appeared to be some measure of language impairment. Not long after she arrived, however, it became known that Genie was actually a thirteen-year-old girl who had been the victim of one of the most severe cases of social isolation in history.

From all available records and accounts Genie had been a normally developing child until just after saying her first words around eighteen months of age. It was at this time that the isolation and abuse began, with Genie spending the next twelve years in the back room of her parents' house, hidden from view. From this point on, Genie was tied to a child's 'potty chair' in nappies and during some nights was bound in a sleeping bag and placed in an enclosed crib with a cover made of metal screening. She was not allowed to speak and her father, who rarely allowed his wife and son to leave the house or even to speak, expressly forbade them to speak to Genie. When Genie did try to speak she was beaten and it was reported that her father would also bark and growl at her like a dog to instil silence. By the time she walked into the social welfare office, Genie was almost entirely mute. And while her vocabulary and comprehension skills improved with years of training after being freed, Genie's grammar and communication skills remained very limited. The lack of language stimulation through normal social interaction from a very young age meant that Genie would never acquire the type of language skills we take for granted. The tragic case of Genie has been supported by volumes of research recognising that the 'learning window' for language requires various types and degrees of stimulation for normal language development to occur with much of this beginning before a child utters its first words.

When babies recognise their native language and begin to babble at around six months of age they are demonstrating the first stages of acquiring language. From six to nine months, infants start to recognise syllables and have begun developing an awareness of phonetic sequences or the sound patterns of their language. At twelve months, a child's understanding of language and perceptions of speech have been dramatically altered by exposure to their native language and by their babbling and rudimentary language skills. However, an ability to make sounds and babble is only part of the recipe for language development. Equally important are the responses a child receives when it babbles and much of this occurs through 'parentese'. While the importance of 'parentese' was mentioned briefly in Chapter Three, the power of 'parentese' requires greater explanation.

If you have never been around grown adults as they speak to infants you may never have heard, 'Helloooo, who's a preeetty baaabeee … oooh, you are sooooo cuuuuute!' Parents, caregivers, immediate family members and even friends will often, and quite naturally, break into this type of speech. This singsong approach to communication is uniquely designed for infants and is evident across most cultures regardless of native language. Like Chomsky's theory of universal grammar, the fact that parentese extends beyond borders and cultural divides has many neuroscientists believing that it too is innate and that it plays a special role in a child's language development. This is due to a number of factors.

Firstly, parentese provides emotional value to sentences and is easily recognisable by its elongated vowels, repetitions and over-pronounced syllables and by its prosody and sound structure. Prosody refers to the emotional quality of speech and it is so important that it can change the entire meaning of a phrase or sentence. For example, 'good for you' or 'good on you' can carry a variety of sentiments depending on how it is said, or its 'prosody'. Parentese is also important for providing infants with their earliest understanding of a language's phonology, morphology, syntax and vocabulary. Professor Steven Pinker, a world renowned experimental psychologist from Harvard University and an expert in many areas concerned with language and the mind, has also discovered that parentese appears to be far more grammatically correct than normal speech and as such offers children their first grammar lessons and the purest forms of initiation into their native language.

Second, although it makes important contributions to language development, parentese also provides children with many examples of important aspects of social interaction. The facial expressions which accompany parentese often include the raising of eyebrows, the wide opening of eyes and the over-emphasis of many facial mannerisms. Emotional expressions found on our faces develop in relation to parentese and the social interactions infants experience also allows for the watching of lip movements, which assists in developing sensitivity to the sounds that accompany those movements. It is important to note that the social signals provided through parentese provide such enriched information for the brain that infants prefer live people in real time over television or other forms of screen interaction. The important message here is that speaking to an infant, especially in parentese, and responding to the babbling and later words they make is far more beneficial to their overall language development then any measure of educational resource or language DVD. Children are drawn to the sounds of their own language and only a short time after birth can discriminate between the real thing and virtual and/or non-speech sounds. Infants need to hear their native language from those closest to them and this continues as children grow older.

While parents are amused when their baby babbles, the second stage of language development sees most parents lose their minds because a baby says its first words. Debates emerge as to whether 'mama' or 'dada' was said first and this important transition from babbling begins between eight and twelve months of age when a child begins to form sounds into words. Those initial words usually fall into two groups. The first of these are objects such as 'cat' or 'juice' and the other group are actions or qualifiers like 'up', 'more' or 'hot'. Adults intuitively realise that single words such as 'juice' might carry additional meaning and stand for something like 'I want juice'. At this stage parentese takes on greater significance but also begins to evolve into increasingly more complex conversations between adult and child.

The third stage of language development emerges at roughly two years of age when children begin to place words together into two-word combinations or phrases. This shift provides parents and adults with a greater understanding of a child's wishes or intent. It is also evidence of a child's growing capacity for identifying actions or relationships when they utter things such as 'juice gone' or 'see dog'. At this time it is also evident that children are developing a growing understanding of grammar and their vocabulary is expanding, all of which continues to evolve until sentences begin to form at around four years of age.

By the time a child reaches four years of age they should be able to articulate their thoughts through short sentences and more sophisticated grammatical structures. Their speech patterns, however, are still somewhat 'telegraphic', which means their speech includes only the words that convey the most meaning and often omits articles ('a' and 'the'), prepositions ('in' and 'out') and parts of some verbs. For example, 'Mummy give milk me' is the telegraphic equivalent of 'Give me the milk, Mummy'. This type of speech is evident for a relatively short time and begins to disappear around five years of age where sentence structure improves indicating that children have learned the basic rules of grammar. The fifth birthday also sees another amazing characteristic of how quickly language develops in the brain. Between two and five years of age a child's vocabulary will have grown from twenty to 50 single words to over 2000 words. This pace of learning new words continues into the school years and can be expanded upon throughout a person's lifetime indicating that learning really can be 'lifelong'.

While expanding on our vocabulary can truly be something done over a lifetime, oral language, in itself, can demonstrate significant variations related to when, exactly, every individual child may move from one stage to the next. Many parents see this through the differences in their own children as they watch them grow and develop. In some instances, children can differ in as much as a whole year in terms of when they pass through a particular stage and much of this depends on the interaction between nature and nurture. None of this is easily predictable or accelerated through extra tuition and/or educational learning tools promoted as mechanisms for enhancing learning or as preparation for academic success. One of the reasons why extra tuition or enhancing literacy through hyper-stimulating language development can be so problematic is that programs and instruments targeting such goals pay little attention to important neurodevelopmental timelines. Concurrently, the progression of sounds and word learning to complex speech is intimately linked with the maturation of Wernicke's and Broca's areas and there are some important facets of this development that no amount of instruction on the road to reading and writing can enhance.

The first thing to note is that Wernicke's area, along with other regions of the brain responsible for language comprehension located towards the back of the left temporal lobe, must develop before Broca's area. This makes sense in that you need to comprehend and understand language before you can put it together. In fact, it appears that the neural layers that facilitate syntax and grammar in Broca's area do not mature until roughly four years of age while full maturation of Wernicke's area is evident by a child's second birthday. Myelination in Broca's area also appears to occur considerably later than in Wernicke's area; myelin is detectable in all cortical layers of Wernicke's area by two years of age in comparison to four to six years of age for Broca's area. Finally, and of major interest to parents and teachers alike, differences in the rates of maturation along with differences in various neuro-anatomical structures and development have been identified between boys and girls.

For a number of years now I have explored and researched gender differences in relation to the brain, learning and behaviour, and I have written about these differences. It is beyond the scope of this book to look at the full range of differences, given that each year the volume of research in this area expands, as do the number of books and articles in this field. However, and without looking at any particular scientific study, most parents and teachers have witnessed differences in the language capacities of boys and girls throughout various stages of childhood. Girls will learn to speak earlier and better than boys, produce longer sentences and demonstrate larger working vocabularies at very young ages. These differences continue throughout the school years whereby girls will typically outperform boys in many facets of language and literacy endeavour while displaying advantages in most aspects of communication. It is also worth mentioning that the neural foundations for gender differences in language are only beginning to be understood and that there are some boys whose language skills are exemplary and some girls who struggle with language and literacy. In essence, the exploration of any measurable gender differences in the brain must be tempered with the realisation that questions of gender differences in language are still largely unanswered and, importantly, not all boys are the same, nor are all girls. At the time of writing, however, what we do know about boys, girls, the brain and language development is interesting enough to consider.

As mentioned earlier, parents and teachers can attest to the fact that they have noticed that the language abilities of girls often appear superior to that of boys and that those abilities and skills are evident early in a child's life. Part of the reason for this could be that the brain processes language somewhat differently in males and females and the regions of the brain responsible for communication not only appear larger in females but also appear to have greater neural density and connectivity. For a number of researchers who specialise in the 'sexually dimorphic brain' (brain differences attributed to sex), one of the most striking differences between the sexes is that language appears to be lateralised somewhat differently in the hemispheres of females and males. Remember, much of our language abilities and capacities occur in the left hemisphere, however the processing of language tends to be equally distributed between both hemispheres in females while language processing in males is done predominantly in the front and back of the left hemisphere. It is also important to note that the dominant language areas located in the left hemisphere appear to mature earlier in girls.

Aside from the important roles of the hemispheres and how language may be processed differently in males and females, there are also some interesting structural differences that may not only impact on the processing of language but also on other important neurological functions. One of the most obvious examples of structural difference and one that is widely debated as the structure that allows females to 'multitask' better than males is the corpus callosum. If you recall from Chapter Two, the corpus callosum is the band of tissue housing a vast array of neural connections linking the hemispheres of the brain. It is, in fact, the bridge between the hemispheres and, as such, it is the primary pathway for communication between the left and right side of the brain. What is interesting about the corpus callosum is that it appears proportionally larger in females. You see, the corpus callosum is actually the same physical size in males and females but because a female brain is physically smaller than its male counterpart, it has greater proportional connectivity. The corpus callosum is also thicker and more bulbous in females and synaptically denser, resulting in a greater number of overall connections between the hemispheres and better 'cross talk' between each hemisphere.

In addition to the proportional size and density of the corpus callosum, two other language-related structures show distinct differences between males and females. Broca's and Wernicke's areas appear to be proportionally larger in females and extensive analyses of Wernicke's area have identified that, in females, the neurons in this region are more densely packed together and have longer dendrites than those of males. Again, if you revisit Chapter Two and how neurons function and communicate, it becomes apparent that more neurons and more dendrites mean greater overall connectivity and proficiency in passing information from region to region. In other words greater neural density and connectivity in particular language regions of the female brain suggests that girls may be afforded greater skills and capacities in areas related to language development and usage as a result of innate sex differences in the brain.

Research into these particular aspects of brain development and gender are still relatively new and often controversial but they are gaining greater recognition as important considerations for child rearing and education. It also stands to reason that if these differences do exist and language development does determine the developmental timelines within and between the genders, then attempts to engage in prescriptive language and/or literacy activities when the brain is not ready for such an endeavour is probably not too dissimilar to having children engage in physical activities when the body is not ready to do so. The important message here is that poorly designed enrichment programs that fail to take into account contemporary theories on how the brain develops may not only be a waste of time but may also do more harm than good. Language development in the brain of a child, be they male or female, does adhere to some particularly important timelines that also rely on certain things to take hold and flourish. Fortunately, you do not need to purchase anything special or have your children enrolled in tutoring for tots ... all you really need is you!

In terms of helping to develop your child's language abilities, let's start by re-emphasising that oral language, and by association language development, is a social activity. Study after study tells us this and that the quality of engagement in conversations, regardless of how rudimentary they might seem, is the fundamental key to healthy and expansive language development. From the earliest stages of life, even the attention given to a baby's babbling is important enough to make a difference in overall language development. As children grow older, the engagement in two-sided conversations becomes a fundamental factor in language development. For example, we know that children as young as eighteen months old will have larger vocabularies than their peers if their parents talked to them about things of interest to that child. We also know that those same children demonstrate larger vocabularies when they enter school and higher levels of reading and maths by the time they are in first grade.

Another important aspect of attending to a child's early verbal meanderings is that while verbal responses are important, facial mannerisms, the emotional quality of responses and social interaction are just as important. In the early stages of life, a child relies on more than just words to build meaning and capacities for understanding and communicating in the world. Language development is assisted by an adult's eye contact and gaze, along with verbal tone and prosody. The social interactions that develop language and that occur between adults and children are about words, sounds, body language, mannerisms and activities in real time rather than anything electronic wrapped up as a toy or tool for language enhancement.

Further important components related to the social foundations of language development include the quantity of words and the quality of conversations. The more words children hear, the larger the vocabulary, and while parentese is important it must also consist of clearly enunciated words. As a child's language capacities improve, the quality of conversation will also improve as long as conversations are two-way interactions. It is important to talk and read to children and tell them stories but it is also very important to listen to children and to get them to talk as much as possible, even when they start asking 'why?' Questions and verbal exchanges are important components of developing a child's overall language capacities and the adults in a child's life would do well to talk about the things children observe and do and, most importantly, build on whatever a child says.

Some final thoughts on language development and brain maturation begin with acknowledging that while the 'learning window' for language lasts roughly ten or eleven years, the most intense and opportune period within this window is in the first six or seven years. The fundamental message is that this timeframe and journey to oral language development requires little more than plenty of talking and social interaction via parents, family and caregivers. Language development flourishes as the brain matures and as it receives its stimulation from human interactions; this is true of all children across all cultures and languages.

Normal and healthy language development is also the precursor to developing all aspects of literacy when a child enters formal educational environments and, as such, should be of fundamental importance to all parents and caregivers. It is now widely accepted that learning to read depends on well-developed language structures and processes in the brain at the nexus of early language experiences. In a cyclical fashion, parents who read to their children from an early age will see their children achieve greater success in learning to read and demonstrate better overall literacy skills as they move through school than those children who seldom or, worryingly, never, received such stimulation. Language development is essential to all aspects of literacy development and school success and can be achieved in the simplest of ways: talk, talk and more talk!

Chapter 8

The emotional and social brain

*Perhaps because it is so much a part of our daily lives, we tend to
take our children's emotional development for granted. Though
we may keep careful track of every motor milestone or vocabulary
addition, we rarely think about the ways in which their emotional
abilities are also rapidly evolving. Yet this aspect of development is
in many ways the most important one of all, because it
establishes the critical foundation on which every
other mental skill can flourish.*

— Lise Eliot, neuroscientist

It is probably a safe assumption that many adults would attest to
the fact that the emotions of a child can be mysterious, puzzling,
beguiling and often just plain tiring. Often those emotions are
displayed in the most public of places. Just about anyone who has
ever visited a supermarket will have seen some children meander
through the aisles as happy little helpers while, in some other aisle,
parents are doing their best to keep a lid on their own emotions while
having to deal with a child in the middle of a tantrum. Puzzling and
tiring indeed!

The emotional development of a child is perhaps the most important foundation for all other types of development. It is intimately linked to social development and considerable volumes of work tell us that regular social interaction is critical to both typical development and adult health. Emotional development is also a crucial consideration with regards to academic achievement and school success. Given the importance of a child's emotions and social interaction and their links to a variety of measures of success in school and later life, the following chapter focuses on the emotional and social development of children during the first few years of life. In order to fully understand these important aspects of development it is best to start with some of the basics related to the emotional structures and systems of the brain.

Chapter Two provided initial insights into the overall structural characteristics of the brain along with a detailed exploration of many of the components that shape our brain and, by extension, our mind, and focused on three significant regions of the brain: the brainstem, limbic system and cerebral cortex. In terms of understanding emotional development, it is the limbic system that is of most interest but a brief review of each region will help frame this chapter.

At the base of the brain is the brainstem. This important region is primarily involved with reflexes and autonomic functions as well as many of our inner drives including hunger and sleep. While you are sitting and reading these pages your heart rate, circulation and breathing are being monitored by the brainstem. This is one of the reasons why a severe enough neck injury can be very problematic or even fatal. Sitting relatively high above the brainstem is the cerebrum, which houses the four lobes of the brain within two hemispheres and is usually identified as the region where thoughtful, organised thinking occurs and the region that separates us from all other living things on Earth. Between, and in the middle of, the brainstem and cerebrum lies the part of the brain responsible for our emotions and various aspects of memory: the limbic system. It is important to remember that overall brain development and maturation occurs from the lower regions of the brain to the higher regions; the lower portions are most developed at birth and overall maturation occurs roughly from the bottom up and from the inside out. This one of the reasons why infants react immediately to environmental stimuli in instinctive or primitive ways while older children or adults may temper any actions with some measure of thought or analysis.

While it is not unusual to segregate and describe the regions of the brain according to their primary function and responsibilities, it is also important to bear in mind that the brainstem, limbic system and cerebrum work in concert with one another and emotions are not solely isolated to the limbic system.

For example, while some regions of the limbic system may be responsible for generating emotions, it is in the cerebrum where feelings of sadness and nervousness, among others, are experienced; the limbic system passes emotional information to the higher order thinking areas where it can be translated into mood, motivation or social awareness. This is an important reminder to parents that our emotional brain is intimately connected to our rational, thinking brain and, as such, emotion and cognition are linked at a neurological level and impact on all aspects of behaviour, thinking and learning. There is a growing mountain of evidence telling us that in terms of basic brain functioning, emotions will often support higher order thinking when they are well regulated, but when emotions are poorly controlled they can also interfere with thinking and, in particular, with attention and decision-making. Of interest to many neuroscientists is the fact that there appears to be more connections running from the limbic system to regions of the cerebrum than there are going in the other direction, suggesting that emotions are often in the driver's seat with regards to our behaviours. Given their potential impact on thinking and overall wellbeing, an understanding of emotions, how they work in the brain and how they develop in childhood, becomes an important consideration for parents.

As puzzling as a child's emotions might be for parents, they are equally puzzling to scientists and theorists. To date, there is little consensus on the nature of emotion and there are many theories with equally as many definitions. For parents it might be easiest to think of emotions as mental or bodily states that can be associated with a wide variety of feelings, thoughts and behaviours. For example, fear may literally make the hair stand up on the back of your neck while sadness may impede you from doing the work your boss needs tomorrow. Arriving at various emotional states requires the use of some important mechanisms of our mind, including physical sensations, perceptions, attention, memory, reasoning and self-reflection. In other words, almost everything we do begins, or is linked, with emotion.

While defining the word 'emotion' may be difficult, the term is often used interchangeably with the word 'feelings'. The two, however, are somewhat different and, as noted above, 'emotions' are the activation of particular perceptual circuits that tell us what we should pay attention to or ignore while 'feelings' are the subjective experiences that emerge from this activation. An example may help to explain this better. If, at this very moment, a loud explosion occurred somewhere outside, your senses would capture that stimulation and your limbic system, working in concert with other regions of the brain, would register an emotional response. That response might then be surprise, anxiety or fear. While this may sound like a simple process, the brain's overall response to unexpected stimuli is not so black and white and is far more complex than easily described in words on a page. This differentiation between emotions and feelings, however, is apparent from the very earliest days in the life of a child.

The brain matures from the bottom up and at birth an infant's limbic system is only partially mature. The important neural connections in an infant's prefrontal cortex will form for about two years before the synapses show maximum density and connectivity. Moreover, the connections that allow greater control of an infant's emotional life will only begin to appear somewhere between six and eight months of age and the communication systems for expressing feelings will emerge some time after that. This is one of the reasons why an infant, or toddler for that matter, will display its feelings very differently to how an adult will. Even a two-year-old with good language skills may not be aware of the emotions it is experiencing or how to express their feelings in a mature way, such as telling someone they feel angry. Interestingly, infants do appear to be able to demonstrate fear responses quite adequately, which may be further evidence of the brain's desire to ensure survival. Babies will also display a number of emotional expressions and appear to have an innate and rudimentary understanding of other people's emotions. You can see this every time a baby smiles, laughs or shows what appear to be expressions of happiness in response to similar stimulation being offered to them; as the months progress, the maturing limbic system and brain will see a great deal of growth in a child's range of emotional expressions.

It is important to remember that in terms of overall development, the first six months of a child's life are dominated by emotional and social development. It's all about survival. Babies need food and security and early infant behaviour is all about meeting those needs via the limbic system. A baby cries when it is hungry, smiles after being fed, and laughs when content; these early emotions and feelings help to shape a child's learned behaviour through the responses it receives. When a baby smiles and an adult smiles back an infant strengthens its understanding of social interactions and learns that certain displays of emotion receive certain types of feedback. In the first six months of life, an infant's smiling and laughing (expressions of happiness and excitement) will be joined by expressions of anger, surprise and sadness. Expressions of fear, shame and shyness seem to emerge between six and eight months and are followed by an expanding emotional repertoire each successive year.

While the first six months of a child's life are an important starting point for survival and the expression of feelings, after six months of age the maturing limbic system, with its growing connectivity to the frontal lobes, facilitates an equally expanding range of expressions and responses to environmental stimuli. Studies using advanced brain-scanning technologies also tell us that increases in the brain's energy consumption, along with growth in dendrites and synapses that coincide with increased myelination in the emotional pathways of the brain, occurs approximately two years after birth. In simple terms this means that at about two years of age the emotional part of the brain and the rational part of the brain begin to communicate together better. As a result of this, children will begin to express their emotions with an increasingly diverse range of facial mannerisms and body language and, as language emerges and develops, feelings will start to be conveyed orally. This also impacts on social development in that toddlers will demonstrate an awareness that other people may have different emotional reactions to their own as well as a growing sense of empathy.

Empathy is a very important part of emotional and social development. When we are empathetic we can sense how someone else might feel which, in turn, allows us to show 'empathetic concern' or 'sympathy'. As babies, we tend to show very primitive notions of sympathy which can, in turn, create headaches for many maternity ward nurses. This is very apparent to anyone who has ever been in a maternity ward when one of the babies begins crying ... once one starts, so do all the others. It is important to remember, however, that this type of empathetic behaviour is involuntary, relies on mimicry and is not indicative of the types of empathetic responses or emotions that require higher order thinking or self-conscious thought. That being said, it is equally important to remember that an adult's response to a crying or smiling infant is believed to be integral in laying the foundations for empathy and concern for others. This is one of the many examples of how nature and nurture work together in sculpting the mind.

While crying babies in a maternity ward may be displaying some measure of empathy, 'true' empathetic behaviour requires us to understand that the 'self' is distinct from other people and that self-awareness begins to emerge roughly around two years of age. A child's capacity for empathy also improves as they mature and come to understand a wider range of emotions and become more adept at assessing other people's feelings. It is worth mentioning that empathy, like many other emotional capacities, does not occur in isolation from other aspects of neurological development. Equally noteworthy is that, although emotional development maintains some general timelines in terms of what one can expect at different ages, overall emotional development, like so many other domains of development, will vary to some degree between all children. With increased age, physical development, movement and independence come diverse experiences which, in turn, also shape the emotional and social brain. Moreover, three important aspects of emotional and social development that become increasingly evident as children become more independent and continue their maturational journey into childhood are 'attachment', 'temperament' and 'emotional regulation'.

Attachment

Attachment is vital to our sense of self and emotional wellbeing. We are by nature social creatures and appear to have an innate need to feel connected, respected and loved by others. This is true even if your teenage sons or daughters give evidence to the contrary by actively disassociating themselves from you, usually when they have friends around. So strong is our need to be connected that many studies have found links between an individual's sense of relatedness and their overall happiness, health and wellbeing. This sense of connection begins early in life and is intimately linked with what has been termed 'attachment'.

The meaning of attachment seems somewhat obvious to most. Attachment relates to a person's emotional bonding with another person or the creation of an enduring emotional tie between two people. Many child development experts and psychologists believe that attachment is perhaps one of the most important aspects of a person's emotional development in that it is the first and principal source of a child's security, self-esteem, self-control and social skills. One of psychology's most prominent researchers in this area was the British psychologist, psychiatrist and psychoanalyst, John Bowlby.

Professor John Bowlby, who was interested in patterns of interactions whether they be healthy or problematic, focused on how attachment difficulties might be transmitted from one generation to the next across a number of families. Bowlby described attachment as a 'lasting psychological connectedness between human beings' and was deeply interested in the important bonds created by children and their caregivers. A central theme to arise from his research was that mothers who are available, caring and responsive to the needs of their infants establish the foundations for attachment, and by association, security and healthy emotional development. It is currently well accepted that security of attachment is not restricted to mothers alone but that it resides in many relationships. Mum is indeed very important, but children will also bond with a variety of people and the nature of those bonds is a product of a child's mind and its environment. In terms of the maturing brain, these bonds begin in the earliest days of life and to some extent can be linked to oxytocin.

Oxytocin is a powerful chemical in the brain. Both males and females have oxytocin but it maintains higher levels in females and is also linked to oestrogen; when oestrogen is high in the monthly cycle so too is oxytocin. Oxytocin also initiates contractions during childbirth and lactation for breastfeeding. It has been referred to as the 'love' or 'bonding' hormone, given its link to various behaviours including sexual and maternal behaviours along with social recognition, memory, pair bonding, trust and attachment. It also appears to be actively released in response to social contact, especially skin-to-skin contact but a fascinating study published in 2010 found that even a simple phone call could alter oxytocin levels and make someone feel better.

In this study, researchers from the Child Emotion Lab at the University of Wisconsin–Madison placed 61 girls, aged seven to twelve, in a stressful situation in order to raise their stress hormones. Don't worry, the stressors were not dangerous or life threatening; instead, the stress these girls endured was facilitated by having to give an impromptu speech and solve maths problems in front of a group of strangers. After performing in front of these strangers, one group of girls was allowed to seek comfort in their mother's arms, another group was allowed to make a phone call and talk to their mothers while the third group was provided with an opportunity to watch an emotionally neutral film, in other words something boring for the respective age group. For the researchers, one of the most fascinating and unexpected findings of the study was that the girls who called their mothers had elevated oxytocin levels similar to that of those who were comforted in person. The researchers were able to determine this because, when elevated, oxytocin helps to diminish the stress hormone cortisol, which can be measured by a simple saliva swab. Researchers have known for quite some time that physical contact increases oxytocin. This study, however, found that the sound of mum's voice, even over the telephone, was enough to elicit feelings of security and comfort and create a neurobiological response to stress by raising oxytocin. Attachment is a very important aspect of emotional and social development and this is evident long before a mother and child can talk over the phone.

In the earliest stages of life, babies are deceptively clever at being comforted and building feelings of attachment with their parents and other family members. They bond quickly with their mothers and during their first few months will also form significant attachments with other members of the immediate family or primary caregivers. However, the type of bonding evident between mother and baby early in life is not apparent between the infant and other adults until some months after birth. Moreover, and in spite of attachment with others, in strange or distressing situations babies tend to prefer their mothers and will generally continue to do so until about eighteen months of age.

At about six months of age, the strong attachment bonds an infant has with its mother and/or primary caregiver are very evident. When separated from mum many babies may appear distressed or anxious or demonstrate what is referred to as 'separation anxiety' or 'stranger fear'. This is a normal emotional milestone and why trying to get a picture with Santa during the festive season will see many babies scream even though mum and dad are just next to the photographer. Grandparents, babysitters and caregivers may fair no better than Santa and children will often cry or show signs of distress with those who may have once comforted them as newborns. In itself, separation anxiety will peak somewhere between ten and eighteen months of age and then begin to fade as a child nears its second birthday.

From two to three years of age attachment is still important to children, however children are now better able to seek contact visually or audibly. In most cases children will, by the age of five, realise that the person or persons they have become so attached to are permanent and they will not need to seek constant contact. It is important to reiterate that, as with all aspects of emotional development, the stages of attachment can also be linked to overall neurological maturation and development. For example, infants demonstrate instinctive characteristics of deriving attachment via crying, cooing and smiling, and much of this is linked to survival and the lower brain regions. As the brain matures so too does a child's memory and capacity to recognise familiar faces. Separation anxiety early in life can be linked to poor memory and immature frontal lobes, which are important mechanisms for recognising object permanence. Object permanence refers to our capacity for understanding that objects or events continue to exist even if they can no longer be heard, touched or seen. You can observe the lack of object permanence in young children by simply hiding something from them in plain sight. Take a rattle or toy they might be playing with and hide it under a tea towel and watch the reaction. Without a sense of object permanence a child who has its toy hidden may become agitated or mildly distressed because they think their toy has completely disappeared. This is because this significant aspect of cognition is not functioning; it requires a maturing memory system and develops slowly.

As noted earlier, it is not until around the age of five that children begin to demonstrate what can be referred to as 'abstract' attachment. A child's attachment with more than one caregiver is obvious as is an understanding that physical contact and/or immediate proximity to those caregivers is not necessary. To that end, the first five years of a child's life are particularly important in terms of creating an environment and the types of social relationships that positively affect attachment and healthy development. Importantly, and although it is difficult to see and we cannot measure attachment in the same way we might measure a child's physical growth, we do know that children who do not form secure attachments early in their lives are more likely to demonstrate various problems throughout childhood and as adults. Low self-esteem, the inability to build and maintain relationships, social and behavioural problems at school and a range of psychological difficulties have been linked to children who begin their lives with compromised or disrupted attachment. It is also important to note that healthy emotional development is also the product of the links between attachment and a child's temperament.

Temperament

It should not be too surprising that temperament is an important aspect of attachment and overall development. A person's own temperament is an integral part of their personality and even infants display unique personality traits from birth. These personalities will impact on relationships, bonding and, by association, attachment. Any parent, perhaps excluding those with identical twins, will tell you that their children can and do display vastly diverse personalities. Some children may be easygoing and appear perpetually happy and content while others struggle to follow a routine and spend a great deal of time with tears running down their cheeks. Individual personalities will, in turn, influence parent–child relationships and parents will handle and respond to different children in different ways; quite often how a parent may respond to a child will be greatly influenced by that child's temperament.

From a psychological standpoint, the term 'temperament' refers to a person's emotional and social style or more precisely the individual differences people demonstrate with regards to attention, emotion, arousal and reactivity to various situations, particularly those that are new or novel. Often, and not unlike the terms 'emotions' and 'feelings', the words 'temperament' and 'personality' are used interchangeably but it is more accurate to note that temperament is only part of a person's personality and that the various characteristics of temperament influence all aspects of development and behaviour. Moreover, while the exact nature of an individual's temperament lacks clear consensus there is substantive evidence that temperament appears to be biologically based and influenced over time by genes, the environment and experience.

A biological or genetic explanation of the differences in temperament help to explain why some children find it difficult to let go of their parent's hand at the door of a kindergarten while others elevate the anxiety levels of their parents when they suddenly disappear in the department store. However, while some aspects of temperament may be innate, the reaction of parents to the sudden disappearance of their child may, in turn, impact on their child's overall temperament. In this sense, and like the emergence of empathy, temperament is another example of the dance between nature and nurture in shaping the mind. Interestingly enough, while our understanding of the neural basis for differences in temperament is still very sketchy, there are some important neurological aspects of temperament worth exploring.

One potential neurological contributor to temperament can be found in the role of particular neurotransmitters. If you recall from Chapter Two, neurotransmitters are the chemical messengers that help facilitate and establish synaptic connections and they play an important role in behaviour. Two neurotransmitters, serotonin and dopamine, appear to play an important part in one's temperament and behaviour and may also be influenced by an individual's environment.

High levels of serotonin have been linked to improved impulse control and reduced aggression while very low serotonin activity has been associated with poor impulse control, increased aggression and greater risk behaviour. Dopamine is an important influence on motivation and novelty-seeking behaviours and this is due to its role in the brain's reward systems. High levels of dopamine activity in certain regions of the brain provide a sense of enjoyment and pleasure thereby increasing the motivation to repeat an experience associated with those feelings. Taken together, and given their influence on how we feel, serotonin and dopamine may play a role in how a child reacts to various stimuli. It is important to mention, however, that while research is making clearer links between neurotransmitters and particular behaviours, neurotransmitters alone cannot explain completely why a child, or an adult for that matter, acts in a particular manner. There appear to be other components of a child's neurological profile that seem to influence behaviour and temperament.

Earlier, reference was made to the fact that the limbic system does not operate in isolation from the rest of the brain and, in particular, to the cerebral cortices that make up the cerebrum. Emotion and cognition collaborate in the processing of information and the display of behaviours and accordingly represent inseparable components of overall development. Three studies that were conducted separately, but focused on looking at the interplay of the prefrontal cortex, emotional regulation, temperament and behaviour, offer evidence of the links between cognition and emotion.

In one study brain activity was measured using electro-encephalograms (EEGs). While looking at brain activity and emotional processing using EEGs, researchers found that the left side of the prefrontal cortex was more active in processing positive emotions related to setting and attaining goals and extroverted behaviour. Quite the opposite was found to be true of the right prefrontal cortex, which appeared more active in withdrawal and negative emotions. These findings suggest that people whose left prefrontal cortex is generally more active tend to be more optimistic and extroverted while those who have greater activity in the right prefrontal cortex appear more pessimistic and withdrawn.

In a different study, still using EEGs, the differences noted above were also identifiable in infant temperament. The researchers in this second study found that infants who cried in response to maternal separation showed greater right frontal activation than those who did not cry. In other words, distressed babies had more going on in their right frontal lobes, the same area associated with withdrawal and negative emotions noted in the previous study. The researchers noted that these differences may be indicative of emotional thresholds for stressful events and that aspects of temperament might be linked to the type and frequency of activity in the right hemisphere of the brain.

In the third related study, EEGs were also used as a mechanism for looking at the cerebral activity of four-year-old children who had been independently identified during playgroup sessions as very outgoing or extroverted and those who demonstrated extremely shy or introverted behaviour two weeks prior to the EEGs. The groups were then broken down into sub-groups where extroverts were identified as 'aggressive' and 'non-aggressive' while introverts were noted as 'fearful' and 'not fearful'. The researchers in this study found that the aggressive extroverts and fearful introverts had greater activity in the right prefrontal cortex while the non-aggressive extroverts and non-fearful shy children had relatively stronger activity in the left prefrontal cortex. Given that the frontal lobes play an important role in self-control and that language is generally housed in the left hemisphere, the researchers in this study suggested that the children who were less aggressive and shy might be able to employ language and other cognitive processes more effectively and, as such, demonstrate overall positive behaviour. Taken in totality, these studies do not mean that a child's behaviour is fixed as a constant throughout life but rather that some children may require different forms of guidance and assistance in coping with their own emotions and temperament given that the response to particular stimuli may elicit different reactions depending on the internal workings of the mind. This is best understood through a child development model looking at notions of temperament and 'goodness-of-fit'.

The temperament of children has long fascinated many and has attracted a great deal of developmental research over many decades. One of the most influential studies to change our understanding of temperament started in 1956 and was published in 1977. This groundbreaking longitudinal study by child psychiatrists Alexander Thomas and Stella Chess followed the lives of 145 children from infancy to adulthood and identified three predominant types of children: 'easy', 'difficult' and 'slow-to-warm-up'. It should not be surprising that many studies since have focused on 'difficult' children given that children who fall into this category also demonstrate a range of behavioural problems. The researchers also found that parenting practices could modify children's temperaments considerably and that temperament can both increase a child's chances of experiencing psychological problems and paradoxically can also protect a child from the toxic environment of a highly stressful home life. From this study, a framework for understanding temperament in terms of a 'goodness-of-fit' model was designed to describe the interplay between temperament and environment, or perhaps it could be considered one of the earliest models of the interplay between nature and nurture.

The 'goodness-of-fit' framework refers to creating child-rearing environments that acknowledge each child's temperament while encouraging more adaptive behaviours and better overall social functioning. This sounds good but it is not always easy. Goodness-of-fit also recognises that temperament can change and this model helps to explain why difficult children may be at greater risk of problems later in life. A difficult child is just that: 'difficult'. Difficult children, in turn, can elicit negative parenting or caregiver interactions resulting in punitive measures to alter difficult behaviour. This can become a vicious circle of anger and/or frustration for both child and parent and we know that angry and punitive discipline appears to undermine the development of 'effortful' control. Studies also tell us that when parents are able to manage their own stress and provide positive, engaging and sensitive interactions this helps children, difficult or not, to better regulate their own emotions. In this sense 'goodness-of-fit' further demonstrates that temperament is a process of nature and nurture and that some approaches to working with children will achieve better long-term results in overall development. This is especially true when these approaches are linked to 'effortful control' or 'emotional regulation'.

Emotional regulation

While attachment and temperament are important, any discussion of emotional development must also regard 'emotional regulation'.

Emotional regulation incorporates notions of 'impulse control' or 'delayed gratification' and is often referred to in a number of different ways including 'self-regulation', 'emotional self-regulation', 'emotional control', 'affect regulation', 'effortful control' and 'emotion management'. It may be easiest to think of emotional regulation as one's ability to manage emotional stimuli effectively and use this purposefully to regulate thinking, learning and our actions: it is the ability to control our behaviours and act in socially acceptable ways. For children, the development of emotional regulation is very important, given that it is a process where children increasingly gain greater control of the behaviours that allow them to achieve functional goals. Therefore, while definitions and references of emotional regulation may differ, they are generally considered a mix of physiological, behavioural and cognitive processes that allow individuals to adjust to experiences.

As alluded to above, emotional regulation is widely regarded as an important objective of a child's social and emotional development and draws a number of links between theories of attachment and temperament. The development of emotional regulation depends on a child's individual, neurobiological and temperamental characteristics along with the types of social interactions that accompany attachment and relationship building. Recent neuroscientific studies suggest that the neural mechanisms underlying emotional regulation may be linked specifically to a number of higher order thinking capacities, including language, sustained attention and working memory. In other words, emotional regulation is linked to a range of cognitive abilities and develops over time.

The regulation of emotions in the early stages of life is assisted by parents and caregivers who control an infant's exposure to events that may be over-stimulating and by comforting and pacifying children through rocking, stroking, holding or singing to them when over-aroused. From roughly six months of age, infants demonstrate that they are making progress at emotional regulation by turning away from unpleasant stimuli or by seeking various objects to suck such as their own thumbs, toys or pacifiers. Your child's attachment to a particular blanket or stuffed animal starts early but as children grow older they will demonstrate a growing array of strategies for avoiding unpleasant stimuli and for achieving desirable outcomes with or without the help of parents and/or caregivers. There is a great deal of improvement in emotional regulation from the ages of three to five and by the time they enter school most children have developed more advanced mechanisms for not only monitoring how well they understand things but also for managing negative emotions appropriately. It should, therefore, not be surprising that emotional regulation is also directly related to a variety of positive educational outcomes.

Over the last ten to twenty years a number of studies have linked emotional regulation with educational outcomes. Taking into account and adjusting for such factors as family income, parent education and the like, children who demonstrate 'good' emotional regulation appear to do better across all aspects of 'schooling', particularly in the early years but also extending into middle school and beyond. Moreover, emotional regulation is a product of nature and nurture and a number of studies examining the relationships between parenting and the development of emotional regulation suggest that adults can positively influence the development of emotional regulation. Significantly, positive emotional regulation has been associated with meaningful praise, sensitivity to a child's needs, security, encouragement, cognitive support, support for autonomous behaviour, a sense of predictability, structure and routine. Conversely, criticism, coldness, indifference to needs, physical or verbal control and lack of structure or routine has been associated with poor emotional regulation. While the factors for enhancing positive emotional regulation appear clear enough, helping children develop positive emotional regulation may not always be as easy as it might seem given the individual nature of each child. However, current research suggests that failure to nurture positive emotional regulation as children grow can have long-term and dramatic consequences, including depression, anti-social behaviour and a variety of psychological disorders. It is, therefore, important to tease out some of the factors noted above and how they influence the positive development of emotional regulation.

First of all, as we now know, the development of emotional regulation is linked to overall brain maturation and especially that of the frontal lobes. In the early stages of life, parents can help build emotional regulation by making sure infants are not overly stimulated. As they grow older infants will begin to mediate their emotions by avoiding sources of too much stimulation, such as loud music or voices. Moving from their first and second birthdays children will voluntarily initiate, maintain and stop behaviours and show aspects of self-control; much of this is learned behaviour acquired through modelling the actions of others. Self-control and improvements in emotional regulation are also evident with improved language whereby behaviour and learning are enhanced through the use of *private speech* directed towards themselves. Young children will regularly talk to themselves as a form of problem-solving and this should never be discouraged given that it is a sign of normal and healthy development. Eventually, as a child matures this private speech becomes internalised and a strong indicator of the brain's maturing cognitive capacities.

While the overall timeline for brain maturation is important in terms of emotional regulation, it is also important to note that this maturational journey does not take place in a vacuum. The environment in which a child grows and lives is just as important to emotional regulation as is its developmental timeline. In terms of the overall environment, positive relationships play an integral role in the development of emotional regulation and an important component of those relationships centres around notions of compliance. When continually forced into compliance by a parent or significant adult, children's emotional regulation can be hindered to some extent in that they are not personally involved in the decision-making process. Studies tell us that children who comply of their own volition or who are provided with reasons for compliance demonstrate positive emotional regulation. It is also important to couple this with the importance of security, structure and routine as noted earlier, in that any rules used as a tool for gaining compliance must be consistent and predictable for emotional regulation to flourish. This cannot be understated given that children will often disagree with requests, rules and decisions and when adults continuously revert to power and control ('Because I told you to!') as a strategy for compliance, rather than consistent rules with explanations, they may be derailing emotional regulation. Moreover, study after study tells us that the most consistent findings in terms of developing positive emotional regulation acknowledge the important role of the care-giving environment. As noted in Chapter Three and indeed throughout most of this book, neurological development thrives when parents and caregivers provide safety, security and minimal stress, and nurture an environment of healthy relationships. Sensitive and responsive parent–child relationships in the home environment have been associated with stronger cognitive skills in young children, fewer behavioural problems, enhanced emotional and social competence and long-term achievement in school. What is important to remember is that 'responsiveness' will vary between adults and children and may need to do so in terms of the different needs of boys and girls.

Not too dissimilar to the sex differences in language development noted in the previous chapter, differences for boys and girls also appear in some aspects of social and emotional development. One of the most important considerations here is that there is growing evidence that these differences are not necessarily a product of nurturing. Continued advances in technology and a growing number of neuroscientific studies tell us that many of the emotional and social differences we see between boys and girls are not the result of being dressed in pink or blue or being given trucks or Barbie dolls to play with. Differences in emotional and social behaviour are evident from birth and some of these differences become more pronounced as children approach the formal years of schooling. That being said, it is also important to bear in mind that while differences between boys and girls are evident, there will also be differences among boys and among girls. Not all boys are the same, nor are all girls, but many of the differences do appear innate due to the fact that they emerge too early in life to be associated with nurturing. For example, we know that as early as one to three days of age, girls are more likely to respond with greater frequency and pay more attention to human voices and faces and are also more likely than boys to exhibit early empathetic behaviours, such as crying in response to another infant's cry. On average, infant girls also make eye contact sooner than boys and hold that eye contact for longer periods of time. Young girls also appear to find faces more emotionally pleasing than boys while boys are more likely to respond to the activities going on around them. One of the reasons that these differences are more nature than nurture may be related to the physical differences in the formation of neurons connected to the retina of the eye in boys and girls. At the risk of oversimplification, girls have a greater number of neurons related to processing colour and the texture of stationary objects that are found in the centre of the visual processing area while boys have larger numbers of a different type of neuron that processes information related primarily to moving objects. In other words, girls appear to have better eyesight and a predisposition for focusing on 'what something is' while boys will focus on 'where something is' or 'where it is going' and both of those are processed in completely different parts of their respective brains.

Early differences in how infant boys and girls might engage with the world around them are also evident in other aspects of early development, including aspects of attachment, temperament and emotional regulation. One of the most noticeable differences between boys and girls is that boys tend to display greater challenges with temperament and emotional regulation. From the very earliest of days, infant boys will often be fussier than girls, fidget more, grimace more, startle more easily, be more irritable, display greater aggressive behaviour and be harder to console when in a state of distress or anger. By the time they are roughly four years old, girls will also appear more emotionally mature in that they show greater ability to self-regulate their emotions and behaviour and process emotional stimuli faster and with greater efficiency. This may be partially related to a girl's earlier proficiency in language skills, as noted in the previous chapter, which allows them to express how they are feeling. Interestingly, childhood problems or disorders related to emotional regulation and overall behaviour such as autism, Asperger's syndrome and attention and conduct disorders are three to four times more likely to occur in boys than girls.

Along with the evidence provided suggesting that sex differences in brain structures may contribute to differences in overall emotional development, differences in maturational timelines of the limbic system that can impact on emotional development are also evident. Different regions of the limbic system appear to mature at different times in boys and girls, which may help to explain greater empathetic behaviour in girls and distinct variations in how boys and girls of the same age may react very differently to emotional stimuli. Many generations of parents and teachers have stated how girls seem to mature sooner than boys and the reasons for this may be as much about the brain as they are about the body. Overall maturation of the brain occurs sooner in females than in males and while full maturation of the brain does not happen until we reach our twenties, the limbic system will mature sooner in girls as will the rest of the regions of the brain. It is, therefore, not surprising that we might see differences between boys and girls when it comes to overall emotional development and, by association, social development.

Social behaviour and the brain

As noted earlier, a girl's proclivity for engaging with faces and people is one of the earliest examples of differences in social development. Differences in social behaviour and how boys and girls engage in group and individual play emerges as early as eighteen months of age. For boys, rough and tumble play becomes a very important aspect of their social life by age three. Rough and tumble play contributes to a boy's social development, can be found in every culture, and is considered a kind of social behaviour that is more nature than nurture. The evidence that rough and tumble may be predisposed to innate sex differences in neurobiology is available when looking at girls born with a syndrome known as congenital adrenal hyperplasia (CAH).

CAH results from a genetic defect where children, both male and female, lack an enzyme needed by the adrenal gland to make the hormones cortisol and aldosterone. In turn, these children are exposed to excessive amounts of testosterone and other androgens (male sex hormones) in the womb. CAH does not appear to have any significant impact on boys but the brains of girls born with this condition appear to become masculinised — CAH girls are more inclined to engage in rough and tumble play, play with 'boy' toys, prefer to play with boys, demonstrate more aggressive behaviour than other girls and are often referred to as 'tomboys'. Even when parents overemphasise and encourage stereotypical girl behaviour or lavishly praise their daughters when playing with 'girl' toys, CAH girls will show little, if any, change in their 'boyish' behaviour. In other words, extensive attempts at nurturing particular types of gender behaviours appear to have no impact on the effect of androgynous hormones on a female brain. Interestingly, CAH girls also perform better on tests of spatial ability than non-CAH girls and as adults CAH girls are more likely to pursue stereotypical 'masculine' careers ranging from truck driving to flying jumbo jets.

The impact of testosterone and other androgens on the brains of CAH girls offers some of the strongest evidence that many of the behaviours we might see in boys and girls are as much a part of the innate differences in the brain as any notion of nurturance or 'upbringing'. Many of these differences are also apparent in adult behaviour and when taken in their entirety the differences noted above suggest that parents, caregivers and teachers would do well to keep in mind that boys and girls may display differences in temperament, attachment and self-regulatory behaviour. It is also important to remember that no single perspective can completely account for all aspects of sex differences in development. Social learning, cognitive development, environmental factors and biology combine to influence the development of most behavioural traits and the current available technology is only beginning to identify the extent of sex differences in the human brain. It is, therefore, important to remember that adults play a critical role in providing the most optimum environment for any aspect of emotional and social development and that, above all else, safety, security and positive relationships are paramount. Many studies have found that the quality and stability of a child's human relationships in the early years lays the foundation for a wide range of later developmental outcomes that really matter and this is abundantly evident when looking at how a child's intellectual capacities emerge and are shaped.

Chapter 9

The birth of intelligence

The problem in conventional assumptions of intelligence is that there is a single measure. People are thought to be more or less intelligent on a single scale based on the ideas of IQ and academic ability. The conventional question to ask of someone's intelligence is 'How intelligent are they?' A more accurate question may be, 'How are they intelligent?'

— Sir Ken Robinson, international advisor on education

How is your child intelligent? This is a very different way of thinking about intelligence and in a world that is changing dramatically at a rate never before seen in the history of humanity it is a very important way of approaching intelligence. One of the reasons why this is so is because many adults across a range of professions continue to cling to notions of intelligence that are arguably outdated. Often intelligence is portrayed as something that you have and/or something that can be improved. These assumptions are both correct and incorrect at the same time. Intelligence is also continuously linked with academic ability and the more intelligence you have, the better. So entrenched are these ideas that an internet search on how to enhance a baby's intelligence or for sites selling products to enhance learning in infants and toddlers can produce millions of hits. After all, most parents want to do as much as possible to ensure that their child is more Einstein than Forrest Gump. Unfortunately the hype surrounding products targeting the building of super brains and the reality are two very different things and while the title of this chapter may suggest that parents can build intelligence in their children, its aim is to discuss some of the problems with such notions and offer a more cautious look at intelligence and brain development. Cautious, because much of what we know about intelligence is speculative and much of what is offered to parents can be very contentious. By way of example, let's look at two common 'neuro-myths' related to early development, the brain and intelligence as touched on briefly in Chapter Five.

One of the most prominent myths presented is that the most important time for learning occurs from birth to age three — the 'myth of the first three years'. This myth is often used to promote products such as early learning tools whereby parents are told that the opportunity for learning is limited and a child's intelligence can be enriched early in life. One of the problems with providing such information to parents is that many of the scientific studies used to support this myth were conducted using non-humans; in fact, most of the studies involved rats in mazes. If you recall from earlier chapters, the brain does require certain types of stimulation for important neural connections to occur. For example, the neural pathways that develop for sight 'expect' that the environment will provide the right type of stimulation at a particular point in time to help build the brain's architecture for sight. However, most of these types of stimulation are available in the day-to-day reality of life and most significantly it is the deprivation of what might be considered 'normal' stimuli that is far more critical than trying to prepare a three-year-old for university. Moreover, while there do exist prime opportunities for certain aspects of learning, these 'windows' of opportunity extend across a number of years and never close completely. You could put this book down at this very moment and go and learn to play the saxophone or speak Russian if you chose to do so.

The second myth is the idea that parents can somehow boost their child's intelligence through 'brain friendly' toys, classical music, DVDs, early enrichment programs or any other commercially prepared teaching and learning tool. In scouring the most current research to date related to the brain, development and learning, the available evidence tells us that the claims of marketing departments and many 'learning' consultants that focus on improving the brain or accelerating learning are founded on studies that have not been tested adequately or in many circumstances have not been tested at all. More worryingly, however, is the existence of well-defined and thoroughly tested research telling us that an overzealous agenda to boost brainpower or intelligence may, in fact, do more harm than good by eroding important aspects of overall development and childhood. To that end it is vital to have a clear understanding of what the word 'intelligence' might mean, explore how it is used, link it to notions of brain development and identify what impacts upon the normal, healthy development of an intelligent mind.

What is intelligence?

As discussed earlier, the word 'intelligence' is rather an elusive concept for it means many things to many people and this has also been mirrored in how it is defined and studied. Many of us often make the mistake of linking the academic achievements of children with intelligence. This is especially true of parents who use report cards to determine how smart their children are or are not. An 'A' means bright and as you move down the list of positive descriptors of intelligence, it diminishes markedly. A person can be described as intelligent in relation to school success, the type of job they have or their professional affiliations, their creative abilities or financial success and, as noted above, the more intelligent a person is, the better. As an aside, different cultures value different types of intelligence and we have also seen the rise of particular notions of 'multiple', 'emotional' and 'social' intelligences in recent times. It is also important to note that intelligence is a product of nature and nurture and, as such, both aspects need to be explored.

In many western societies, the most familiar and widely accepted descriptions of intelligence are those linked to cognitive abilities or factors thought to be involved in intellectual performance. We often assess how intelligent people are by how well they perform in things we hold as valuable and then associate this with innate qualities of the mind. In the early 1900s, an English psychologist by the name of Charles Spearman played a part in constructing our notions of intelligence as an innate ability. Spearman developed a description of intelligence as an innate 'general mental ability' or 'the g factor' that could be measured, which is what most contemporary IQ scores derive from.

Around about the same time that Spearman was developing his theory of intelligence, a French psychologist by the name of Alfred Binet was devising a test that would be used to help identify those children who might not be able to learn in school and could then be sent to special schools. Binet's work resulted in the first intelligence test, which has since been modified on a number of occasions and is still used today to provide IQ scores. These scores are based on comparisons with other people and are represented in a graph that looks a lot like a camel's hump. Most people (about 68 per cent) will score somewhere within the hump and between a range of 84 and 116; roughly 15 per cent will score on one side of the hump or the other. In other words approximately seven out of ten people will have similar or 'normal' IQ. Those outside of the hump will either be below 'normal' intelligence, as seen in individuals with Down's syndrome, or they will be above average intelligence and, depending on the score, may even be described as a genius. For parents it is also important to remember that while IQ tests can help in distinguishing mental retardation from normal intelligence in babies and young children, it cannot distinguish moderate differences in intelligence within this age bracket. IQ scores become stable throughout childhood, are fairly reliable around age eight and will settle around adult scores somewhere around the twelfth birthday. It is also important for parents to bear in mind that many IQ tests are culturally biased and often only indicative of the types of learning a child has received in school; as such, they are not always good determiners of overall intelligence.

While the work of Spearman and Binet has been very influential in the fields of psychology and education, another important player in our understanding of the nature and nurture of intelligence is

Raymond Cattell. Cattell was an English and American psychologist who expanded on Spearman's notion of general mental abilities and argued that general intelligence is actually a conglomeration of many abilities that work together in various ways to bring out different intelligences that can broadly be separated into 'fluid' and 'crystallised' intelligences. For Cattell, fluid intelligence represented a person's innate abilities to detect relationships among various stimuli and to process this information effectively, efficiently and quickly. Fluid intelligence is all about a person's ability to think and act quickly, or to reason, and it is an innate capacity grounded most noticeably in the brain (nature). Crystallised intelligence, on the other hand, represents those skills and abilities we get from accumulated knowledge and experience, good judgement and social skills, and stems from learning and the environment (nurture).

The reason for embarking on a discussion of Cattell's work is that it helps to illustrate a number of important considerations related to intelligence and the development of intelligence or cognitive abilities in children. First, and not too dissimilar to IQ, fluid intelligence is presented as something innate, which will vary between individuals and, importantly, it will change over time due to maturation. Second, crystallised intelligence is a product of the environment and the learning experiences children will have. Third, some types of testing studies have shown that children who possess similar 'fluid' intelligences but come from different cultural backgrounds perform differently on 'crystallised' tasks. In other words, any test that aims to identify a measure of intelligence must be scrutinised carefully to ensure that it does not disadvantage individuals due to their social, economic and/ or cultural context. Children, and adults for that matter, will often demonstrate other notions of intelligence beyond the scores offered in pencil and paper tests. And finally, the fluid nature of intelligence is an important consideration with regards to the brain and the overall nature of intelligence in children. This is particularly evident if we consider that fluid intelligence is linked to brain maturation or what psychologists and child development experts refer to as 'cognitive development'.

Cognitive development and intelligence

Cognitive development and intelligence are intimately linked and you would be hard pressed to find anyone who disagrees with the notion that children grow smarter as they grow older. Years of research have demonstrated that a child's ability to understand abstract concepts and perform certain cognitive tasks is directly related to brain maturation and improves with age. For parents it is also important to look at the links between brain maturation and the 'nature' of intelligence before looking at how to nurture cognitive development and intelligence in a healthy and positive fashion.

Throughout most of the chapters of this book aspects of brain development related to intelligence and cognitive development have been presented. Chapters Three, Four and Five provided specific insights into brain maturation, age-related abilities and the types of skills and attributes a parent might expect to see of their child at particular points in time. The information below adds to this by providing further insights into overall brain maturation and 'intelligence' by examining how a preschooler's brain is able to perform far more complex tasks than that of a newborn child.

It is quite obvious and should not be of any surprise that newborns may not appear very intelligent in comparison to older children. There are three important reasons why this is so and they are related to 'mental speed', overall neural efficiency and the maturation of the brain's frontal lobes. At birth the brain has very few neural connections and runs relatively slowly. This does not mean that newborn babies are not engaged in intelligent activities, only that they are engaged in what we might call 'immature' intelligent activities. Newborns are very active in soaking up information through all of their senses and, as noted earlier, are able to recognise a mother's voice and use this to also recognise her face. Newborn babies are also capable of distinguishing certain speech sounds and prior to their first birthday demonstrate aspects of reasoning, categorisation and abstraction. For example, studies have shown that one-month-old babies can match the feeling of something they suck on in their mouths with a picture of that object. These early skills are some of the many surprising abilities researchers have discovered in the last decade supporting the theory that the building blocks for higher cognitive processes are innate and improve with age. Further evidence of improved cognition is also evident in IQ tests where scores improve and become progressively more stable with age.

As noted above, improvements in cognitive development are evident as the brain matures and becomes faster at performing mental tasks. The brain of a newborn baby responds to sensory stimulation anywhere from three to four times slower than that of an adult but this will increase dramatically in the first year when the production of myelin is rampant and sees a two- to threefold increase in the acceleration of neural transmission before a child's tenth birthday. This increase in speed also means that the brain becomes more efficient as it matures through childhood in that it will be better equipped to process, store, retrieve and analyse information and it will also burn less energy in doing all of those important cognitive tasks. This is one of the amazing paradoxes related to brain maturation: in spite of an infant's slower processing speed, it uses far more energy than an adult brain. Scientists believe that this is most likely due to the overproduction and then later pruning of synaptic connections which, in itself, contributes to greater neural connectivity, efficiency and overall cognitive abilities and intelligence.

Notwithstanding the important implications of brain speed and efficiency, the maturation of the frontal lobes is also a very important aspect of cognitive development and intelligence. The frontal lobes are one of the last regions of a baby's brain to form while in the womb, and during childhood the frontal lobes form and prune synapses more slowly than any other region of the brain. Full maturation of the frontal lobes, in particular the prefrontal cortices, does not occur until we become adults and this maturational journey is a neurobiological inevitability for all humans and cannot be sped up or advanced. Given that the frontal lobes play a role across a range of cognitive capacities including reasoning, abstract thought, managing conflict, self-regulation of emotions, working memory, paying attention and concentrating on tasks, it should be apparent that the maturational timeline of the frontal lobes places limitations on a range of intellectual abilities in children. Couple this with all of the other factors discussed above and it becomes clear that any notion of intelligence must take into account how the brain matures. For example, studies tell us that various aspects of fluid intelligence related to reasoning ability emerge somewhere between a child's second and third birthday, growing steadily until middle childhood and then more slowly until plateauing during adolescence. Keeping all of this in the forefront of our own minds, here are a few neurologically influenced milestones we would expect to see in normal children.

The first year of life is mostly about the senses. This is a time of sensory-dependent activity and infants and toddlers will learn a great deal simply from engaging with the world through their senses. At around eight months of age, the frontal lobes become far more active allowing for the development of increased performance in working memory, self-regulation, attention, concentration and greater goal-directed activity due to improvements in motivation. Children at this age will reach for things and pay more attention to the dancing seahorses twirling on the mobile above them. There are also greater connections being made between the frontal lobes and limbic system and, as a result, attachment emerges as an important aspect of both emotional and cognitive development. These connections between the rational and emotional brain are also related to improvements in executive attention, which begins to emerge in the second year of life and allows children to tell the difference between various things and focus their attention on people or other things important to them.

During this time of improved connectivity there is also an increase in the growth of dendrites in the left hemisphere of the brain at roughly eight months of age and this growth corresponds to the emergence of language. Not long after their first birthday, a child's improving language skills provides evidence of the most obvious change in a child's cognitive capacities. The emergence of language is also a contributing factor to a range of other cognitive, emotional and social capacities. Children are better able to engage in symbolic thought and have increased levels of self-awareness along with increasingly sophisticated levels of engagement with other people as they become more independent. Symbolic thought allows people to use words or symbols to express concepts such as 'mother' or extend thoughts beyond concrete objects by making abstract references to the future. In a cyclical fashion this increasing independence, along with opportunities for greater social engagement, appears to act as a 'gate' to further language development in that children strive to communicate as much as possible. The reciprocal nature of language development is further evidence of the interconnections between the nature and nurture of cognitive, emotional and social development discussed throughout this book.

While language is a distinct marker of brain maturation, as children move from toddlerhood into their third and fourth year, the brain is still continuing to develop. One of the most significant changes to occur is that communication between the hemispheres of the brain improves markedly due to myelination in regions that allow for greater crosstalk between the right and left hemispheres. As infants, the right hemisphere appears more dominant and while the left hemisphere becomes more prominent at age two, it is not until about four years of age that the integration of a child's analytical/linear (left) hemisphere and intuitive/spatial (right) hemisphere takes place. At this point in time a child's brain now resembles that of an adult's in terms of how the hemispheres function. It is also at this time that memory improves markedly and children become more aware of their own perceptions and begin to demonstrate that they know what might be going on in someone else's mind or what is referred to in psychology texts as 'theory of mind'. This ability to understand and predict another person's mental processes including their thoughts, emotions, motives, beliefs and intentions will continue to mature and develop as children enter formal schooling and sometime around their sixth birthday their intellectual and cognitive abilities will reach new heights.

Around six years of age, children will be demonstrating greater degrees of cognitive sophistication. They will have greater powers of attention, concentration, self-regulation and emotional control. This emergence of higher cognitive skills at this age occurs across all cultures and is yet another indicator of innate neurological maturation. Jean Piaget, one of history's most well-known child development psychologists, who continues to have a tremendous influence in schools, referred to this time as a period of 'operational thinking'. Long before we could use technology to look into a child's mind, Piaget found that at this point of their lives children's thinking and reasoning becomes logical, their working memory improves and they begin to demonstrate that they can perform higher order cognitive activities such as classifying objects mentally. By the time they reach school most aspects of memory improve and children become increasingly more proficient at encoding, storing and retrieving memories whether they be episodic, procedural or semantic. You can refer back to Chapter Six if you cannot retrieve your own semantic memories regarding each type of memory just mentioned!

One other thing to mention regarding the brain at six years of age is that it is during this time that the vast neural networks across all regions of the brain demonstrate greater efficiency and speed. This is also a period that signals the beginning of the end of synaptic proliferation as the brain starts to move into a new phase of development that will see your child's brain being altered a great deal once pubescence takes hold. And while the brain will continue to mature into adulthood, many aspects of the mind, cognition and intelligence are now reaching a point where the immediate impact of nurturing in the early years begins to wane. Indeed, nurturing intelligence happens long before a child begins formal educational and as such requires some explanation and clarification.

Whenever any discussion on how parents might nurture their child's intelligence is presented, an immediate problem arises, given the understandable aspirations of parents and teachers alike, who strive to make kids 'smarter'. As noted earlier, a great deal of hype surrounding such aspirations has resulted in a wide range of products and profit-generating industries targeting learning and young children with promises of making kids more intelligent. In most western countries intelligence is regularly viewed as a type of commodity and the more that you have of that commodity the better. It is, therefore, very important to re-emphasise that the idea that any product can enhance intelligence or cognitive capacity is not supported by any substantive research and, in itself, demonstrates a lack of intelligence with regards to the brain and child development. You need not look at the studies to verify this but rather consider that most parents can attest to the fact that children will often ignore the toys they receive as gifts while they find ways to play with the wrapping paper or climb inside the box that housed the toy itself. Children learn from exploring, playing and making sense of the world and intelligence is not something that can be easily programmed or enhanced. However, current research tells us that there are some environmental factors that do seem to impact on overall aspects of cognitive development and intelligence. Many of these factors have already been noted at various junctures throughout this book but the fundamental foundations supporting all that has been discussed is presented below.

It cannot be stated enough that the most important factor related to cognitive development and intelligence is that children require safe and secure environments and need to be surrounded by positive, loving relationships. Intelligence is not developed through instructional DVDs or early learning toys but can be nurtured through responsive, nurturing relationships with parents, caregivers and teachers. Study after study tells us that the key predictors of healthy intellectual development are found in the relationships between children and those responsible for their care and wellbeing and that this is particularly true in the earliest years of life. Moreover, the survival needs of an infant necessitate social interaction and the quality of these interactions influences cognitive development. Some researchers believe that the links between breastfeeding and IQ as discussed earlier may have less to do with the potential nutrients in breast milk and more to do with the quantity and quality of the social interaction that occurs between mother and baby. So important are relationships that vision, hearing, language, attachment, temperament, emotional regulation and all other aspects of development thrive in social environments that are safe, caring and supportive, and there is little doubt that healthy cognitive development and intelligence are also part of this nurturing equation.

As children move from infancy to toddlerhood to school, they become more independent and mature and consequently their relationships change and evolve. As children move from one birthday to the next they engage with the world and the people around them in increasingly sophisticated ways. It is important to remember, though, that their young brains are still immature and tend to operate in survival mode and because of this immaturity children also require predictability and consistency from the adults around them. Children also need the adults around them to show patience when mistakes are made and encouragement when first attempts do not go according to plan. A good part of intelligence in relation to healthy cognitive development is nurtured through exploration and opportunities to extract meaning from such explorations and more often than not it is the mistakes that children make that provide a great deal of meaning and intellectual stimulation. When we try to make our children perfect and stigmatise their mistakes we may hinder various aspects of cognitive development as it may lead a child to become passive and overly risk averse. Children learn and develop when they are encouraged to explore and when they are supported when trouble arises. They also thrive and are more likely to try new things or have another go at something gone wrong if we praise their effort and not their intelligence. Praising effort is a powerful motivator because effort is something that can be changed. In our society, telling a child they have succeeded at something because they are smart sets them up for internalising potential mistakes or failures as a product of them being not so smart, or dumb!

Notwithstanding the important link between relationships, cognitive development and intelligence, it is also important to note that the nature of relationships will, and must, vary with age and within home and school contexts. As children gain greater independence and confidence the adults around them begin to have increasingly important roles in helping them make sense of the world. Nowhere is this more apparent than when children embark on some measure of formal schooling. What happens in preschool, kindergarten and the early days of primary school in conjunction with what teachers do 'with' or 'to' children is an area where neuroscience and our understanding of the human brain can be most informative. The next and final chapter of this book provides some further insights into your child's developing brain and what the science tells us is important to remember when children go to school.

Chapter 10

The developing brain goes to school

Academic preschools that emphasise learning over play have become popular because parents want to make sure their children get a leg up in life. Life is tough; no question about it. But it's just not true that the best kind of learning takes place only when a big, smart adult directs the child's every move ... years of research have shown that children need to direct their own play activities. When children have a chance to play, they show an increase in creativity and problem solving.

— Kathy Hirsh-Pasek, professor of psychology, and Roberta Michnick Golinkoff, professor of psychology and linguistics

Life is tough and we are busy! Sound familiar? How many times do we lament that we are so busy or that we just can't seem to get on top of things. It's all about the future, isn't it? We work hard to get ahead in preparation for something better and we prepare our children for the future so that they can also get ahead. We want the best for our kids and too often this translates into having children do more sooner or finding ways to build their résumés earlier. In many respects schools have fallen into this trap as well and are pressing academic demands on children at very young ages. Some schools pay little, if any, attention to developmental timelines and are engaging four- and five-year-olds in rigorous academic instruction beyond their capabilities. It is also not uncommon for four-year-olds to be given considerable amounts of homework because there is a pervasive belief that more is better or that preparation for university begins shortly after toilet training. Life can be busy, but that does not mean that this should be so for our children.

From the very first pages of this book there have been a number of inferences highlighting a worrying trend of having young children do too much too soon. There are a number of potential factors that have contributed to this and while many generations of child development experts have argued for developmentally appropriate schooling, a new era of mind/brain science adds much weight to that position. However, one of the interesting paradoxes to emerge from neuroscientific research has also seen the proliferation of a number of dubious platforms for building better brains during the early years of childhood. This chapter begins by revisiting some earlier points related to all areas of development. It then looks to expand on those ideas with a view to offering insights into what parents and teachers alike should focus on in terms of the developing brain and raising healthy, happy and 'educated' children. The place to start this discussion is to reiterate what is best for children before they ever step into some type of school.

Throughout this book it has been noted that the optimum conditions for healthy neurological development in the earliest days of life requires that children be fed, feel safe and secure and to be loved. This is about survival and once those needs are met children also need to grow in an environment where relationships are healthy and positive and where stress is kept to a minimum. A child's brain is an amazingly perceptive device and can sense fear, tension and stress long before it can articulate those perceptions or feelings. We are born to survive and learn, in that order, and young children arrive with innate capacities for taking in sensory information and reacting to it. Time and time again the most important message to emerge from many fields of study related to child development is that the greatest single determinant in healthy neurological development is that of a positive loving relationship with parents and/or primary caregivers.

The benefits of positive relationships

Because positive relationships are so important, it is not uncommon for many people to ask, okay, what constitutes a positive relationship? This is a good question and one that has received a great deal of attention in recent years. There are a number of characteristics that provide the framework for positive relationships and each one is important. Firstly, and albeit rather obviously, children must be protected from harm and unforeseen threats. Second, and somewhat related to the previous characteristic, relationships must be reliable, consistent and predictable in order for confidence and trust to flourish between a child and its caregiver. Third, how an adult responds to a child is important. Many aspects of a child's emotional development will be shaped by how parents and caregivers respond to the needs and desires of a child; love and affection helps to develop self-esteem and self-worth. This also means that parental patience and support for the growth of new skills and capabilities within a child's reach is positive and forgiving when necessary. If nothing else you should remember that children are not little adults, their brains are maturing and changing which means their immature memory systems, attention and ability to concentrate will impact on what they say and do. This leads onto the fourth important characteristic, which is best described as the provision of opportunities to experience and resolve conflict cooperatively. Learning is a form of reciprocal interaction and children learn the importance of mutual give-and-take through cooperation and resolving differences respectfully. Finally, the young mind of a child needs the experience of being respected by others and opportunities to demonstrate respect for others. Children develop and learn in a world of mimicry and modelling and in the words of my grandfather, whom I loved dearly and learned a great deal from as a child, 'Monkey see, monkey do'!

Safe and secure environments along with positive relationships are the foundations of healthy brain development and once these are in place most aspects of development and learning will flourish. Earlier chapters in this book looked at a number of insights into specific notions of neurological development related to learning, language, emotional and social development and intelligence. Significantly, and in spite of all the hype related to learning toys and enrichment, the greatest opportunities children have for learning and preparing for school occur though the everyday experiences they have with their parents or caregivers. Children can learn about shapes when meals are prepared and slices of cheese are transformed from squares to triangles. When children go outside they learn about textures from feeling grass and rocks and, if mum and dad can cope with the mess, from dirt and mud. Children learn the differences between sweet and sour the first time they have an ice cream or taste a lemon and they quickly learn that putting a bug in the mouth is 'yucky'. When children cross the street they learn about care and caution and their language skills are enhanced when adults tell them to look both ways. Household items such as pots and pans, wooden spoons, plastic containers and cardboard boxes provide hours of self-indulgent fun and myriad learning opportunities. Yes, toys do provide learning opportunities but parents do not need to visit toy stores in search of early learning enhancers when the home has many safe things that will interest a child. Indeed, the home and outside world are awash with many types of stimulation but it is also important to remember that too many toys, too many people or too much stimulation can be just as problematic as too little. The developing brain also needs downtime as much as it needs experiences to wire up its neural circuits. Fortunately, children are quite adept at letting us know how they feel and that they need downtime through an array of behaviours; being agitated or overly fussy are good examples of when a child needs downtime. Moreover, opportunities to rest and be idle are an important way to recharge and the developing brain needs constant recharging.

While parents and the home provide a great deal of stimulation, it is also vital that a great deal of learning develops in social contexts. A child's self-confidence grows when it begins to crawl, walk, feed itself, talk and engage in increasingly complex relationships. Children learn how to make friends and get along with others by watching their parents and through the day-to-day interactions they have with the people around them. They develop self-regulatory behaviours and learn self-control when they have to wait their turn to go down the slippery slide or when they stand in line with mum or dad at the supermarket. Their self-control and temperament are further enhanced through consistent and predictable environments and through watching how the adults around them mediate stress and those difficult moments in parenting that might be called 'childhood mistakes' or, perhaps more appropriately, 'learning opportunities'. So important are social skills and self-control that a great deal of evidence tells us that not only can these capabilities be shaped by experience but that they are also major contributors to overall intellectual achievement and a happy and successful life.

The social contexts children engage in not only assist in many aspects of development but they often provide opportunities for a great deal of physical activity. Aside from proper nutrition and getting enough sleep, the developing brain of a child also needs to be physically active. Yes, activity is important for the body and for encouraging positive lifestyle choices but there is also a considerable amount of research showing that exercise and physical activity is not only important for the body but also for healthy brain development. Exercise improves aerobic fitness, and aerobic fitness in children has been linked to improved perceptual skills, verbal ability, mathematical ability, school readiness, attention, self-control and aspects of memory. Some of the strongest links between all of these and brain development occurs in children between the ages of four and seven. Exercise is such a powerful influence on the brain that many studies have identified that exercise can impact on the physical size of certain structures in the brain and cause the release of proteins that support the growth of dendrites, synapses and increased synaptic density. Fortunately, during the early years of development, children rarely need any encouragement to move or be active but it may be wise to carefully monitor the time spent on computers and watching television as children grow older. Remember that children's brains are optimised to learn from social interactions and this is especially true of infants and toddlers. Moreover, there isn't any reliable evidence that technology can take the place of real life or that television has any benefits for babies while television, DVDs and learning videos appear to have little place in the life of children prior to their second year. In fact, researchers have found the risks of developing attention problems at age seven increase in relation to the amount of television watched between one and three years of age. Research has even found connections between the time spent watching baby DVDs and declines in the pace of language development. In one particular study researchers noted that while daily reading with a parent can be associated with a seven-point increase in language scores across various measures, each hour of daily baby DVD viewing was associated with a seventeen-point decrease. The take-home message here is to remember that early in life children learn a great deal from real-world experiences through interactions with real people.

Notwithstanding the potential problems associated with products marketed to enhance learning in young children, opinions related to older children, learning and television or other sources of audiovisual material vary quite markedly. It is also important to remember that most people find things they like about television and it is therefore rather unrealistic to try to completely ban television viewing as much of what children might see may occur incidentally. It is also very difficult to classify television or various forms of media as entirely 'good' or 'bad'. For example, some studies have found that *what* children watch is just as important as to whether they watch anything or not. In one study researchers found that exposure to *Dora the Explorer* led to an increase in vocabulary and expressive language skills in two-year-old children while similar exposure to the *Teletubbies* resulted in a decrease in both areas. The most significant message from these types of studies appears to be that, comparatively speaking, all aspects of learning and development thrive through the real-life interactions a child has over those found through television, videos and 'brain-building' toys or interactive media.

The real-life interactions children have early in life change in frequency and quality as they grow older and enter formal schooling. Schools provide children with new opportunities to learn and grow considerably as they engage with new people and new environments. These new opportunities, however, must always bear in mind that children do not need to be 'prepped' to learn, but they do need to learn in ways that are developmentally appropriate and structured around the best available research related to learning and teaching.

Long before researchers could look at the inner workings of the brain, psychologists, teachers and other professionals had been designing learning environments for children. Kindergarten is one such environment. The first kindergarten, or 'children's garden', was founded by Friedrich Froebel in Germany in 1937. Froebel was a teacher who believed that children should be led according to their own interests and be free to explore those interests through 'self-activity'. In this setting a teacher was there to guide and the learning environment was to be a thriving garden of opportunity. Today, the term kindergarten is now widely known in most western countries and it generally marks some aspect of 'schooling' prior to entry into the first formal year of schooling or Year One. Currently, and depending on context, there now exists a number of avenues for children to engage in educational endeavour prior to Year One, be it through 'kindergarten', early learning centres, 'preschool' and/or 'prep'. In terms of the kinds of activities that should occur within these environments, the word 'play-based' often emerges.

Play to learn

The importance of play in relation to learning has a long history dating as far back as Plato in ancient Greece. There has been a great deal of research conducted looking at various aspects of play, and today 'play' is generally recognised as an important component of learning and teaching. However, while play has a long history of importance in terms of early learning and development, it is often not well understood in many public domains. Perhaps one of the biggest reasons for this is a belief that if a child is playing, then they are not working and surely to learn something we must work at it. In fact, far too many parents and school systems often naively neglect the play needs of children and assume that learning in children and adults occurs in a similar fashion. For adults, learning something new can often lead to some degree of work or applied effort and so this must be true of children as well. The importance of play to a child's cognitive development may also be taking a back seat to other notions of 'schooling' given what appears to be an increasing emphasis on accountability and testing. Unfortunately, adult notions of learning and schooling often fail to take into account the wealth of research saying that play is important to healthy brain development, especially in the early years of schooling. Here are some of the things that the research tells us about play.

First and foremost, study after study has identified that throughout their school lives children do better academically and socially when they come from a home and early learning environments that fostered a great deal of play and exploration. Play is a means of engaging and interacting with the world, and through play, children learn to conquer their fears and build new competencies that lead to enhanced confidence and resilience. Through play children also develop language and problem-solving abilities, expand their creative capabilities, improve their social skills, enhance their memory capacities and perhaps, most significantly, reduce any levels of stress. Play comes naturally to children and one of the reasons play offers so much in terms of learning and development is that it is usually fun!

Pleasure and fun are powerful motivators! When children, or adults for that matter, engage in playful behaviour identified by the brain as pleasurable, a number of regions in the brain explode into action. The activation of these regions leads to the release of some very influential chemicals that not only contribute to repetitive behaviours but also facilitate learning at a synaptic level. Repetition is important to learning and children are more likely to repeat pleasurable activities which, in turn, leads to remembering and learning from these repetitive behaviours. Remember that, from a neurological standpoint, repetition strengthens synaptic connections and stronger connections mean better neural connectivity, which means that the brain can spend more energy on new learning and the refinement of other synapses. In other words, practice not only makes perfect, it makes connectivity permanent. Moreover, the 'fun' factor of play also allows children to learn what they like and don't like while trial and error, problem solving, imagination, creative endeavour, language skills and most other aspects of overall development are enhanced through play.

While all play generally entices children to engage in pleasurable activities, some types of play may be more cognitively beneficial than others. Social and emotional skills developed through play are usually observable when watching children engage with one another. However, in terms of specific aspects of cognitive development there are particular types of play that prove more beneficial and assist in the development of self-regulation. Remember that self-regulatory behaviour refers to the ability of the frontal lobes to manage one's emotions, urges, impulsive behaviours and the capacity to control attention and other cognitive processes. Self-regulation has also been linked to overall school success whereby children who have poorly developed self-regulatory behaviours struggle in the academic and social confines of formal schooling. Recent studies have found that the more children indulge in particular types of pro-social play, the sooner and more completely they will develop frontal lobe regulatory functions.

Throughout this book the importance of providing developmentally appropriate opportunities for learning has been discussed. You might think that, given that the brain's prefrontal cortices do not fully mature until we are in our twenties, it would seem unlikely that they can be enhanced. However, a child's frontal lobes do mature and with the appropriate level of support and planning, self-regulation and other aspects of executive functioning can be strengthened before children enter their first year of primary school. A number of programs and schools have looked at the research supporting such claims and one in particular has seen remarkable success.

'Tools of the Mind' is an early childhood program originating in the United States that has gained a great deal of recognition, given its success at enhancing self-regulatory behaviour in young children. At the core of the program is an approach to working with children in a way that promotes and fosters mature dramatic play. For 'Tools of the Mind', mature dramatic play is all about providing opportunities for children to engage in extended make-believe scenarios lasting for extended periods of time. Importantly, when children participate in dramatic play, the teachers play a role coordinating, facilitating and supporting imaginary scenarios that children choose to participate in and fall into particular roles guided by social norms. Literacy and numeracy strategies are also incorporated into play scenarios with a view to improving many important skills, including oral language, knowledge of letters, familiarity with the conventions of print, counting meaningfully, one-to-one correspondence, patterns and number recognition. The emphasis, however, is on self-regulatory behaviour which is fostered when children assume an imaginative role, such as pretending to be an airline pilot. They must behave in ways that meet the social rules of that role and rely on private or internal speech to help define the role. Children also learn to curb impulses in order to think about how they might act and what they might say while role-playing. Programs like 'Tools of the Mind' and others that engage in mature dramatic play have made important contributions to our understanding of particular types of play in that children who engage in this type of activity show improvements in self-regulatory behaviour, aspects of executive functioning, language capacities and overall school readiness.

While mature dramatic play offers an important component of early education, it is also significant to note that not all play must be structured with a view to attaining some predetermined outcome. Unstructured or 'free' play is also important for social, emotional and cognitive development as well as for emotional wellbeing. Free play rarely has a predetermined set of rules and, as a result, it provides children with opportunities to engage in creative responses and challenges the developing brain to use its imagination. The lack of predetermined rules and structures in free play also facilitates problem-solving behaviours. When children decide what to play, who can play, when to start, when to stop and the rules of the game, they are promoting the use of the higher order thinking parts of the mind. Free play also provides children with opportunities to develop greater sophistication in their language skills. During moments of free play, children often talk to each other about things that may not be physically present and their levels of symbolic, functional and oral language are more varied and complex in peer play compared to when they are interacting with adults. Last, but certainly not least, free play allows children to experience the pleasures associated with movement, creativity and relationships and consequently maintains a number of, as yet, unmeasurable attributes that can only be seen as positive contributions to overall development.

The pleasurable aspects of play, whether derived from mature dramatic play facilitated by adults or as a result of unstructured free play, are important components for healthy brain development. These types of activities are also complimentary to the term '*preschool*'. It is only some time after a child's fifth birthday that the brain is emotionally and cognitively ready for the types of formal learning that occurs from Year One and throughout primary school. When children make the transition from 'preschool' environments, and barring any developmental problems, they generally do so with a brain that is more mature and better equipped to deal with the types of learning and expectations they will encounter in Year One. By the time they approach six years of age children become better able to learn on demand, follow adult reasoning, use memory in a deliberate fashion, grapple with more abstract concepts and demonstrate increasingly better self-control to sit for longer periods of time while attending to what is being taught. However, this is not to say that by the time they enter Year One the mind of a child is anywhere near fully mature. Learning is a lifelong process and schools must do everything they can to ensure that learning environments match the developmental needs of children regardless of age. Failure to do so can lead to one final important consideration regarding the developing brain and school.

The important links between healthy brain development and safe, secure and supportive environments have been noted on a number of occasions throughout this book. In the earlier chapters, the debilitating effects of stress on the brain were also noted. Stress is also an important consideration when children enter school environments and while it is true that a child's cognitive capacities improve as they grow older, it is also true that the emotional part of the brain can directly impact on thinking, learning and development. Therefore, any environment designed as a place of learning must do all it can to ensure that it is not only safe and supported but also as devoid of stress as possible.

Stress is a killer! For adults, stress-related disorders include depression, alcoholism, obesity, suicide and drug addiction to name a few. Stress also hinders the immune system, is linked to high blood pressure and strokes and has been noted as the greatest contributor to cardiovascular disease. Novelty, unpredictability, situations deemed threatening and the lack of a sense of control provide the perfect ingredients for the brain to engage in a stress response. Moreover, one of the reasons stress can have such a powerful impact on children is that their developing brains are far more sensitive to the chemical processes involved while mediating a stressful event. Not all stress is detrimental but negative stress (distress) can be very destructive considering how it engages the parts of the brain that trigger the very mechanisms which ensure our survival.

Whenever the brain goes into a state of distress it tells the hypothalamus to release powerful chemicals and stress hormones that initiate a series of reactions so the body can prepare for fight or flight. Interestingly, two areas of the brain that play a major role in learning, memory and emotional responses, the hippocampus and amygdala, can be adversely effected by stress and, in particular, by chronic stress. Furthermore, when engaged in situations eliciting a sense of fight or flight, the stress hormone cortisol can even shut down our capacity to think. The elevation of cortisol is one way our brain ensures its focus is on survival and reacting to the situation at hand. This is one of the reasons why, sometimes after a stressful event, we have greater clarity of thought and often think to ourselves, 'Why didn't I say this?' or 'Why didn't I do that?' This phenomenon, known as 'downshifting', results from elevated cortisol which literally shuts down higher order thinking and other normal cognitive capacities so we can focus on surviving. Chronic stress and prolonged elevated cortisol levels in adults have also been linked to the physical shrinking of the hippocampus, as documented in individuals suffering from post-traumatic stress disorder. Given that stress can have such a devastating impact on the mature mind of an adult, its impact on children cannot be understated. And whether chronic or not, stressed children are less likely to show curious, risk-taking, exploratory or novelty-seeking behaviours. Considering that learning environments are generally founded on fostering creativity, thinking and learning in relation to cognitive endeavour, it should be evident that such environments are emotionally responsive to children and as stress-free as possible. Moreover, the most resounding finding from numerous stress-related studies is that parents, caregivers and teachers are the most significant players when it comes to stress management in children.

One final note! Being a stress manager and meeting the emotional needs of children is not only important in terms of responding to particular emotional states or reducing stress. When children engage in learning within relaxed environments and feel less overwhelmed, studies tell us that their brains function better. When teachers and learning environments are consistent, predictable, positive, warm and appropriately responsive to emotional cues, children also display fewer negative behaviours, less time off task, more self-reliance and greater self-regulation. Importantly, when schools overly emphasise logical reasoning or the accumulation of factual knowledge, which are often the most measured indicators of educational success, they fail to appreciate that emotions are a critical force in learning. Educating and raising children consists of a social contract between children and adults. This social contract requires careful consideration of how a child's brain matures and develops. In the twenty-first century, parents, caregivers, teachers and all those who work with children now have far greater insight into the inner workings of a child's mind. In the future our understanding of the brain will surely grow and should help ensure that adults use their minds as effectively as possible to make sure that everything they do with, and to, children is all about the developing brain and nurturing healthy minds.

Acknowledgements

My intent in writing this book was to offer parents, teachers and all those who work with children some insights into how a child's brain develops and how it can be influenced by so many things other than just its genetic makeup. As part of this I am hoping that the information presented might prove useful and, at times, inspire those who read its pages to be the best parents and/or teachers possible. It is in this context that I would like to express my gratitude to the many individuals who have inspired, encouraged and supported me to be the best parent and educator I can be prior to, and while writing, this book.

This list begins with Emily and our children, Madeline and Harrison. Emily's support in all that I have set out to do is second only to her love and support for our children and all that they aspire to be. Without realising it, my two beautiful children, Maddie and Harry, have taught me a great deal about childhood and as they grow older I am confident that they will continue to teach me so much more.

I would also like to recognise a number of people who have inspired my own notions of parenting and who are the types of nurturing parents this book could use as examples of how to raise healthy and happy children: Brett and Sharon Schimming, Kristine Jenkins, Bryan and Lillian Hicks, Enio and Leeanne Ricci, Reg and Rhonda Grainger, Dan Kahan, Yvette Andre and Paul and Fiona Clark.

Inspirational people often leave long-lasting memories in the grey matter of our own psyche and two such individuals continue to do so for me. As someone who grew up and went to school in Canada, I was fortunate in having two particular teachers who nurtured me during important years of my life. As an adult, my respect for them is such that, to this day, I cannot refer to them by their first names but revert back to Mr Borys and Mr Neiles. Barry Borys and John Neiles taught me the meaning of the words perseverance, dedication and hard work and also to always believe in myself. To this day they influence how I act as a parent, coach and educator.

Finally, I want to thank my family back in Canada. My parents, Albert and Janet, helped to form a great part of who I am and I would not be doing what I am doing if not for them. It is not always easy being a little brother, but my brother Bill has survived that role and is a well-loved brother, husband, father, coach and teacher. Last, but by no means least, it is with much love that I acknowledge my sister Donna who became a parent early in life and is now the loving mother of two beautiful daughters and an inspiration for all who are lucky enough to know her.

References

Ahola, D & Kovacik, A. (2007). *Observing and Understanding Child Development: A Child Study Manual*, Thomson Delmar Learning, New York.

Allred, LW. (2007). *Piggyback Rides and Slippery Slides: How to Have Fun Raising First Rate Children*, Cedar Fort Inc, Springville, Utah.

American Academy of Pediatrics. (2009). *Caring For Your Baby and Young Child: Birth to Age Five*, 5th edn, Bantam, New York.

Andersen, BB, Korbo, L, & Pakkenberg, B. (1992). A quantitative study of the human cerebellum with unbiased stereological techniques. *Journal of Comparative Neurology*, 326, 4, 549–560.

Anderson, JW, Johnstone, BM & Remley, DT. (1999). Breast-feeding and cognitive development: A meta-analysis. *American Journal of Clinical Nutrition*, 70, 4, 525–535.

Anderson, DR & Pempek, TA. (2005). Television and very young children. *American Behavioral Scientist*, 48, 5, 505–522.

Bailey, R. (2006). Physical education and sport in schools: A review of benefits and outcomes. *Journal of School Health*, 76, 8, 397–401.

Balog, D (ed.). (2006). *The Dana Sourcebook of Brain Science*, 4th edn, Dana Press, New York.

Barnett, WS, Jung, K, Yarosz, DJ, Thomas, J, Hornbeck, A, Stechuk, R & Burns, S. (2008). Educational effects of the Tools of the Mind curriculum: A randomized trial. *Early Childhood Research Quarterly*, 23, 3, 299–313.

Baron-Cohen, S. (2003). *The Essential Difference: The Truth About the Male and Female Brain*, Basic Books, New York.

Bauer, PJ. (2005). New developments in the study of infant memory. In DM Teti (ed.), *Blackwell Handbook of Research Methods in Developmental Science*, pp. 467–488, Blackwell Publishing, Oxford.

Bavelier, D, Green, CS & Dye, MWG. (2010). Children, wired: For better and for worse. *Neuron*, 67, 5, 692–701.

Beard JL & Connor JR. (2003). Iron status and neural functioning. *Annual Review of Nutrition*, 23, 41–58.

Begley, S. (2007). *Train Your Brain, Change Your Mind: How a New Science Reveals Our Extraordinary Potential to Transform Ourselves*, Ballantine Books, New York.

Bell, MA & Wolfe, CD. (2004). Emotion and cognition: An intricately bound developmental process. *Child Development*, 75, 2, 366–370.

Bellisle, F. (2004). Effects of diet on behaviour and cognition in children. *British Journal of Nutrition*, 92, supp 2, 227–232.

Benjamin, J, Ebstein, RP, & Belmaker, RH (eds.). (2002). *Molecular Genetics and the Human Personality*, American Psychiatric Publishing Inc, Washington.

Ben-Yehudah, G & Fiez, JA. (2007). Development of verbal working memory. In D Coch, KW Fisher & G Dawson (eds.) *Human Behavior, Learning and the Developing Brain: Typical Development*, pp. 301–328, The Guilford Press, New York.

Benenson, JF. (1993) Greater preference among females than males for dyadic interaction in early childhood. *Child Development*, 64, 2, 544–555.

Benenson, JF, Apostoleris, NH & Parnass, J. (1997). Age and sex differences in dyadic and group interaction. *Developmental Psychology*, 33, 3, 538–543.

Benson, AM & Lane, SJ. (1993). The developmental impact of low level lead exposure. *Infants and Young Children*, 6, 2, 41–51.

Bergen, D & Coscia, J. (2001). *Brain Research and Childhood Education: Implications for Educators*, Association for Childhood Education International, Olney, Maryland.

Berk, L. (2006). *Child Development*, 7th edn, Allyn and Bacon, Boston.

Berninger, VW & Richards, TL. (2002) *Brain Literacy for Educators and Psychologists*, Elsevier Science, San Diego.

Best, JR, Miller, PH, & Jones, LL. (2009). Executive functions after age 5: Changes and correlates. *Developmental Review*, 29, 3, 180–200.

Biddle, SJH, Fox, KR, & Boutcher, SH. (2001). *Physical Activity and Psychological Well-Being*, Routledge, London.

Bjorklund, DF. (2005). *Children's Thinking: Cognitive Development and Individual Differences*, Wadsworth/Thomson Learning, Belmont, California.

Black, JE, Jones, TA, Nelson, CA & Greenough, WT. (1998). Neuronal plasticity and the developing brain. In JD Noshpitz, NE Alessi, JT Coyle, SI Harrison & S Eth (eds), *Handbook of Child and Adolescent Psychiatry — Volume 6: Basic Psychiatric Science and Treatment*, pp. 31–53, Wiley, New York.

Blair, C. (2002). School readiness: Integrating cognition and emotion in a neurobiological conceptualization of children's functioning at school entry. *American Psychologist*, 57, 2, 111–127.

Blair, C & Razza, RP. (2007). Relating effortful control, executive function, and false belief understanding to emerging math and literacy ability in kindergarten. *Child Development*, 78, 2, 647–663.

Blakemore, SJ & Frith, U. (2005). *The Learning Brain: Lessons for Education: A précis*. Blackwell Publishing Limited, Oxford.

Bloom, FE, Beal, MF & Kupfer, DJ (eds.). (2006). *The Dana Guide to Brain Health: A Practical Family Reference from Medical Experts*, Dana Press, Washington.

Bodrova, E & Leong, DJ. (2005). Uniquely preschool: What research tells us about the ways young children learn. *Educational Leadership*, 63, 1, 44–47.

Bodrova, E & Leong, DJ. (2007). *Tools of the Mind: The Vygotskian Approach to Early Childhood Education*, 2nd edn, Prentice Hall, Columbus, Ohio.

Bowlby, J. (1969). *Attachment and Loss, Volume 1: Attachment*, Basic Books, New York.

Brazelton, TB & Greenspan, SI. (2000). *The Irreducible Needs of Children: What Every Child Must Have to Grow, Learn and Flourish*, Perseus Books Group, Cambridge, Massachusetts.

Brizendine, LB. (2006). *The Female Brain*, Morgan Road Books, New York.

Brizendine, LB. (2010). *The Male Brain*, Broadway Books, New York.

Brody, LR & Hall, JA. (2000). Gender, emotion and expression. In M Lewis & JM Haviland-Jones (eds.) *Handbook of Emotions*, 2nd edn, pp. 338–349, The Guilford Press, New York.

Brody, N. (1997). Intelligence, schooling and society. *American Psychologist*, 52, 10, 1046–1050.

Brown, S. (2009). *Play: How it Shapes the Brain, Opens the Imagination, and Invigorates the Soul*, Penguin Books, New York.

Bryan, J, Osendarp, S, Hughes, D, Calvaresi, E, Baghurst, K, & van Klinken, JW. (2004). Nutrients for cognitive development in school-aged children. *Nutrition Reviews*, 62, 8, 295–306.

Burdette, HL & Whitaker, RC. (2005). Resurrecting free play in young children: Looking beyond fitness and fatness to attention, affiliation, and affect. *Archives of Pediatrics and Adolescent Medicine*, 159, 1, 46–50.

Bush, G, Luu, P & Posner, MI. (2000). Cognitive and emotional influences in anterior cingulate cortex. *Trends in Cognitive Sciences*, 4, 6, 215–222.

Byrnes, JP. (2007). Some ways in which neuroscientific research can be relevant to education. In D Coch, KW Fisher & G Dawson (eds.), *Human Behavior, Learning and the Developing Brain: Typical Development*, pp. 30–49, The Guilford Press, New York.

Cahill, L, Haier, RJ, White, NS, Fallon, J, Kilpatrick, L, Lawrence, C, Potkin, SG & Alkire, MT. (2001). Sex-related difference in amygdala activity during emotionally influenced memory storage. *Neurobiology of Learning and Memory*, 75, 1, 1–9.

Cahill, L. (2005). His brain, her brain. *Scientific American*, May, 40–47.

Cahill, L. (2006). Why sex matters for neuroscience. *Nature Reviews Neuroscience*, 7, 6, 477–484.

Caine, G & Caine, RN. (2001). *The Brain, Education, and the Competitive Edge*, The Scarecrow Press Inc, Lanham, Maryland.

Calvin, WH & Ojemann, GA. (1980). *Inside the Brain: Mapping the Cortex, Exploring the Neuron*, New American Library, New York.

Calvin, WH. (1996). *How Brains Think: Evolving Intelligence, Then and Now*, Weidenfeld & Nicolson, London.

Canli, T, Desmond, JE, Zhao, Z & Gabrieli, JDE. (2002). Sex differences in the neural basis of emotional memories. *Proceedings of the National Academy of Sciences*, 99, 16, 10,789–10,794.

Carey, J (ed.). (2008). *Brain Facts: A Primer on the Brain and Nervous System*, The Society for Neuroscience, Washington DC.

Carew, TJ and Magsamen, SH. (2010). Neuroscience and education: An ideal partnership for producing evidence-based solutions to guide 21st century learning. *Neuron*, 67, 5, 685–688.

Carnegie Corporation of New York. (1994). *Starting Points: Meeting the Needs of Our Youngest Children: The Report of the Carnegie Task Force on Meeting the Needs of Young Children*, Carnegie Corporation, New York.

Carter, R. (2000). *Mapping the Mind*, Orion Books Ltd, London.

Carter, R. (2009). *The Human Brain Book: An Illustrated Guide to Its Structure, Function and Disorders*, Dorling Kindersley Limited, London.

Casey, BJ, Giedd, JN & Thomas, KM. (2000). Structural and functional brain development and its relation to cognitive development. *Biological Psychology*, 54, 1 & 3, 241–257.

Castelli, DM, Hillman, CH, Buck, SM, Erwin, HE. (2007). Physical fitness and academic achievement in third- and fifth-grade students. *Journal of Sports and Exercise Psychology*, 29, 2, 239–252.

Cattell, RB. (1971). *Abilities: Their Structure, Growth and Action*, Houghton Mifflin, Boston.

Cattell, RB. (1987). *Intelligence: Its Structure, Growth and Action*, Elsevier Science Publishers, New York.

Chabris, C & Simons, D. (2010). *The Invisible Gorilla and Other Ways Our Intuition Deceive Us*, Crown Publishers, New York.

Chaddock, L, Erickson, KI, Prakash, RS, VanPatter, M, Voss, MW, Pontifex, MB, Raine, LB, Hillman, CH & Kramer, AF. (2010). Basal ganglia volume is associated with aerobic fitness in preadolescent children. *Developmental Neuroscience*, 32, 3, 249–256.

Chaddock, L, Hillman, CH, Buck, SM & Cohen, NJ. (2011). Aerobic fitness and executive control of relational memory in preadolescent children. *Medicine and Science in Sports and Exercise*, 43, 2, 344–349.

Chomsky, N. (1957). *Syntactic Structures*, Mouton Publishing, The Hague.

Christakis, DA, Zimmerman, FJ, DiGiuseppe, DL & McCarty, CA. (2004). Early television exposure and subsequent attentional problems in children. *Pediatrics*, 113, 4, 708–713.

Chugani, HT. (1994). Development of regional brain glucose metabolism in relation to behavior and plasticity. In G Dawson & KW Fischer (eds.) *Human Behavior and the Developing Brain*, pp. 153–175, Guilford Press, New York.

Chugani, HT. (1997). Neuroimaging of developmental non-linearity and developmental pathologies. In RW Thatcher, GR Lyon & J Rumsey (eds), *Developmental Neuroimaging: Mapping the Development of Brain and Behavior*, pp. 187–195, Academic Press, Inc, San Diego, California.

Chugani, HT. (1998). Biological basis of emotions: Brain systems and brain development. *Pediatrics*, 102, 5, 1225–1229.

Chugani, HT. (2004). Fine-tuning the baby brain. *Cerebrum*, 6, 3 (Summer), 33–48.

Chugani, HT, Phelps ME & Mazziotta JC. (1987). Positron emission tomography study of human brain functional development. *Annals of Neurology*, 22, 4, 487–497.

Chugani, HT, Phelps ME & Mazziotta JC. (1989). Metabolic assessment of functional maturation and neuronal plasticity in the human brain. In C von Euler, C Forssberg & H Lagercrantz (eds.), *Neurobiology of Early Infant Behaviour, Wenner-Gren International Symposium Series*, 55, pp. 323–330, Stockton Press, New York.

Cicchetti, D, Rogosch, FA Gunnar, MR & Toth, SL. (2010). The differential impacts of early physical and sexual abuse and internalizing problems on daytime cortisol rhythm in school-aged children. *Child Development*, 81, 1, 252–269.

Cirulli, F, Berry, A & Alleva, E. (2003). Early disruption of the mother–infant relationship: Effects on brain plasticity and implications for psychopathology. *Neuroscience and Biobehavioral Reviews*, 27, 1 & 2, 73–82.

Cole, PM, Michel, MK & Teti, LO. (1994). The development of emotion regulation and dysregulation: A clinical perspective. *Monographs of the Society for Research in Child Development*, 59, 2 & 3, 73–100.

Cole, PM, Martin, SE & Dennis, TA. (2004). Emotion regulation as a scientific construct: Methodological challenges and directions for child development research. *Child Development*, 75, 2, 317–333.

Colonnesi, C, Draijer, EM, Stams, GJJM, Van der Bruggen, CO, Bogels, SM & Noom, MJ. (2011). The relation between insecure attachment and child anxiety: A meta-analytic review. *Journal of Clinical Child and Adolescent Psychology*, 40, 4, 630–645.

Conlan, R (ed.). (1999). *States of Mind: Discoveries About How Our Brains Make Us Who We Are*, John Wiley & Sons Inc, New York.

Connellan, J, Baron-Cohen, S, Wheelwright, S, Batki, A & Ahluwalia, J. (2000). Sex differences in human neonatal social perception. *Infant Behavior and Development*, 23, 1, 113–118.

Crain, W. (2003). *Reclaiming Childhood: Letting Children Be Children In Our Achievement-Oriented Society*, Henry Holt & Company, New York.

Crugnola, CR, Tambelli, R, Spinelli, M, Gazzotti, S, Caprin, C & Albizzati, A. (2011). Attachment patterns and emotion regulation strategies in the second year. *Infant Behavior & Development*, 34, 1, 136–151.

Cullen, KE & Roy, JE (2004). Signal processing in the vestibular system during active versus passive head movements. *Journal of Neurophysiology*, 91, 5, 1919–1933.

Curtiss, S. (1977). *Genie: A Psycholinguistic Study of a Modern-Day 'Wild Child'*, Academic Press, New York.

Cycowicz, YM. (2000). Memory development and event-related brain potentials in children. *Biological Psychology*, 54, 1 & 3, 145–174.

Cynader, MS & Frost, BJ (1999). Mechanisms of brain development: Neuronal sculpting by the physical and social environment. In DP Keating & C Hertzman (eds.), *Developmental Health and the Wealth of Nations*, pp.153–184, Guilford Press, New York.

Damasio, AR. (2000). *The Feeling of What Happens: Body and Emotion in the Making of Consciousness*, Harcourt Inc, New York.

Damasio, AR. (2004). Emotions and feelings: A neurobiological perspective. In ASR Manstead, N Frijda & A Fischer (eds.), *Feelings and Emotions: The Amsterdam Symposium (Studies in Emotion and Social Interaction)*, pp. 49–57, Cambridge University Press, Cambridge.

Davidson, RJ. (1992). Anterior cerebral asymmetry and the nature of emotion. *Brain and Cognition*, 20, 1, 125–151.

Davidson, RJ & Fox, NA. (1989). Frontal brain asymmetry predicts infants' response to maternal separation. *Journal of Abnormal Psychology*, 98, 2, 127–131.

Davidson, RJ, Lewis, DA, Alloy, LB, Amaral, DG, Bush, G, Cohen, JD, Drevets, WC, Farah, MJ, Kagan, J, McClelland, JL, Nolen-Hoeksema, S & Peterson, BS. (2002). Neural and behavioral substrates of mood and mood regulation. *Biological Psychiatry*, 52, 6, 478–502.

Davis, CL, Tomporowski, PD, McDowell, JE, Austin, BP, Miller, PH, Yanasak, NE, Allison, JD & Naglieri, JA. (2011). Exercise improves executive function and achievement and alters brain activation in overweight children: A randomized, controlled trial. *Health Psychology*, 30, 1, 91–98.

De Bellis, MD, Keshaven, MS, Beers, SR, Hall, J, Frustaci, K, Masalehdan, A, Noll, J & Boring, AM. (2001). Sex differences in brain maturation during childhood and adolescence. *Cerebral Cortex*, 11, 6, 552–557.

Decety, J & Michalska, KJ. (2010). Neurodevelopmental changes in the circuits underlying empathy and sympathy from childhood to adulthood. *Developmental Science*, 13, 6, 886–899.

Dehaene-Lambertz, G. (2000). Cerebral specialization for speech and non-speech stimuli in infants. *Journal of Cognitive Neuroscience*, 12, 3, 449–460.

Denham, S. (1998). *Emotional Development in Young Children*, The Guilford Press, New York.

Dewey, J. (1938). *Experience and Education*, Collier Books, New York.

Diamond, A. (2000). Close interrelation of motor development and cognitive development and of the cerebellum and prefrontal cortex. *Child Development*, 71, 1, 44–56.

Diamond, A, Barnett, WS, Thomas, J & Munro, S. (2007). Preschool program improves cognitive control. *Science*, 318, 5855, 1387–1388.

Diamond, M & Hopson, J. (1999). *Magic Trees of the Mind: How to Nurture Your Child's Intelligence, Creativity, and Healthy Emotions from Birth Through Adolescence*, Penguin Putnam Inc, New York.

Dickerson, SS & Kemeny, ME. (2004). Acute Stressors and Cortisol Responses: A Theoretical Integration and Synthesis of Laboratory Research. *Psychological Bulletin*, 130, 3, 355–391.

Dixon SD. (2006). Understanding children: Theories, concepts and insights. In: Dixon SD & Stein, MT (eds.), *Encounters With Children: Pediatric Behavior and Development*, 4th edn, pp. 12–43, Elsevier Mosby, Philadelphia.

Dondi, M, Simion, F, & Caltran, G. (1999). Can newborns discriminate between their own cry and the cry of another newborn infant? *Developmental Psychology*, 35, 2, 418–426.

Dowling, M. (2010). *Young Children's Personal, Social and Emotional Development*, 3rd edn, Sage Publications, London.

Dwyer, T, Sallis, JF, Blizzard, L, Lazarus, R, Dean, K. (2001). Relation of academic performance to physical activity and fitness in children. *Pediatric Exercise Science*, 13, 3, 225–237.

Edelman, GM 2006, *Second Nature: Brain Science and Human Knowledge*, Yale University Press, New Haven, Connecticut.

Eigsti, IM, Zayas, V, Mischel, W, Shoda, Y, Ayduk, O, Dadlani, MB, Davidson MC, Aber, JL & Casey, BJ. (2006). Predicting cognitive control from preschool to late adolescence and young adulthood. *Psychological Science*, 17, 6, 478–484.

Eisenberg, N, Fabes, RA, Guthrie, IK, & Reiser, M. (2000). Dispositional emotionality and regulation: Their role in predicting quality of social functioning. *Journal of Personality and Social Psychology*, 78, 1, 136–157.

Eisenberg, N & Morris, AS. (2002). Children's emotion-related regulation. In R Kail (ed.), *Advances in Child Development and Behavior*, 30, pp. 189–229, Academic Press, San Diego.

Eisenberg, N, Valiente, C & Eggum, ND. (2010). Self-regulation and school readiness. *Early Education & Development*, 21, 5, 681–698.

Eliot, L. (2000). *What's Going On in There? How the Brain and Mind Develop in the First Five Years of Life*, Bantam Books, New York.

Elkind, D. (1982). *The Hurried Child: Growing Up Too Fast, Too Soon*, Addison-Wesley Pub Co, Reading, Massachusetts.

Elkind, D. (1987). *Miseducation: Preschoolers at Risk*, Alfred A. Knopf Inc, New York.

Engle, RW, Kane, MJ & Tuholski, SW. (1999). Individual differences in working memory capacity and what they tell us about controlled attention, general fluid intelligence, and functions of the prefrontal cortex. In A Miyake & P Shah (eds.), *Models of Working Memory: Mechanisms of Active Maintenance and Executive Control*, pp. 102–134, Cambridge University Press, New York.

Eveland-Sayers, BM, Farley, RS, Fuller, DK, Morgan, DW, Caputo, JL. (2009). Physical fitness and academic achievement in elementary school children. *Journal of Physical Activity and Health*, 6, 1, 99–104.

Faull, J & McLean-Oliver, J. (2010). *Amazing Minds: The Science of Nurturing Your Child's Developing Mind With Games, Activities and More*, Berkley Books, New York.

Feldman, R, Eidelman, AI, Sirota, L & Weller, A. (2002). Comparison of skin-to-skin (kangaroo) and traditional care: Parenting outcomes and preterm infant development. *Pediatrics*, 110, 1, 16–26.

Felitti, VJ, Anda, RF, Nordenberg, D, Williamson, DF, Spitz, AM, Edwards, V, Koss, MP & Marks, JS. (1998). Relationship of childhood abuse and household dysfunction to many of the leading causes of death in adults: The adverse childhood experiences (ACE) study. *American Journal of Preventative Medicine*, 14, 4, 245–258.

Fifer, WP & Moon, CM. (1995). The effects of fetal experience with sound. In J Lecanuet, WP Fifer, N Krasnegor & WP Smotherman (eds.), *Fetal Development: A Psychobiological Perspective*, pp. 351–367, Lawrence Erlbaum Associates Inc, Hillsdale, New Jersey.

Fisher, KR, Hirsh-Pasek, K, Golinkoff, RM & Gryfe, SG. (2008). Conceptual split? Parents' and experts' perceptions of play in the 21st century. *Journal of Applied Developmental Psychology*, 29, 4, 305–316.

Fox, NA. (1991). If it's not left, it's right: Electroencephalograph asymmetry and the development of emotion. *American Psychologist*, 46, 8, 863–872.

Fox, NA, Schmidt, LA, Calkins, SD, Rubin, KH & Coplan, RJ. (1996). The role of frontal activation in the regulation and dysregualtion of social behavior during preschool years. *Development and Psychopathology*, 8, 1, 89–102.

Fox, SE, Levitt, P, and Nelson, CA. (2010). How the timing and quality of early experiences influence the development of brain architecture. *Child Development*, 81, 1, 28–40.

Frank, DA, Klass, PE, Earls, F & Eisenberg, L. (1996). Infants and young children in orphanages: One view from pediatrics and child psychiatry. *Pediatrics*, 97, 4, 569–578.

Freud, S. (1905/1963). Introductory lectures on psychoanalysis. In J. Strachey (ed.) *The Standard Edition of the Complete Psychological Works of Sigmund Freud*, pp. 199–201, Hogarth Press, London.

Friederici, AD. (2006). The neural basis of language development and its impairment. *Neuron*, 52, 6, 941–952.

Fries, ABW & Pollak, SD. (2007). Emotion processing and the developing brain. In D Coch, KW Fisher & G Dawson (eds.), *Human Behavior, Learning and the Developing Brain: Typical Development*, pp. 329–361, The Guilford Press, New York.

Froebel, F. (1895). *Pedagogics of the Kindergarten: Or, His Ideas Concerning Play and Playthings of the Child*, D Appleton & Company, New York.

Galsworthy, MJ, Dionne, G, Dale, PS & Plomin, R. (2000). Sex differences in early verbal and non-verbal cognitive development. *Developmental Science*, 3, 2, 206–215.

Garrett, B. (2009). *Brain and Behaviour*, 2nd edn, Sage Publications, Thousand Oaks, California.

Gathercole, SE. (1999). Cognitive approaches to the development of short-term memory. *Trends in Cognitive Sciences*, 3, 11, 410–419.

Gazzaniga, MS. (1985). *The Social Brain*, Basic Books, New York.

Gazzaniga, M. (1998). *The Mind's Past*, University of California Press, Berkeley, California.

Gazzaniga, M, Heatherton, T & Halpern, D. (2010). *Psychological Science*, 3rd edn, W.W. Norton & Company, New York.

Geary, DC. (1998). *Male, Female: The Evolution of Human Sex Differences*, American Psychological Association, Washington DC.

Geary, DC. (2002). Sexual selection and sex differences in social cognition. In AV McGillicuddy-De Li & R De Lisi (eds.), *Biology, Society, and Behavior: The Development of Sex Differences in Cognition*, pp. 23–53, Ablex/Greenwood, Greenwich, Connecticut.

Geary, DC, Byrd-Craven, J, Hoard, MK, Vigil, J & Numtee, C. (2003). Evolution and development of boys' social behaviour. *Developmental Review*, 23, 4, 444–470.

Georgieff, MK. (2007). Nutrition and the developing brain: Nutrient priorities and measurement. *The American Journal of Clinical Nutrition*, 85, supp 2, 614–620.

Gervai, J. (2009). Environmental and genetic influences on early attachment. *Child and Adolescent Psychiatry and Mental Health*, 3, 25, 1–12.

Giedd, JN, Vaituzis, C, Hamburger, SD, Lange, N, Rajapakse, JC, Kaysen, D, Vauss, YC & Rapoport, JL. (1996). Quantitative MRI of the temporal lobe, amygdala and hippocampus in normal human development: Ages 4–18 years. *Journal of Comparative Neurology*, 366, 2, 223–230.

Giedd, JN, Blumenthal, J, Jeffries, NO, Castellanos, FX, Liu, H, Zijdenbos, A, Paus, T, Evans, AC & Rapoport, JL. (1999). Brain development during childhood and adolescence: A longitudinal MRI study. *Nature Neuroscience*, 2, 10, 861–863.

Giedd, JN. (2004). Structural magnetic resonance imaging of the adolescent brain. *Annals of the New York Academy of Sciences*, 1021, 77–85.

Giedd, JN. (2010). The teen brain: Primed to learn, primed to take risks. In D Gordan (ed.). *Cerebrum: Emerging Ideas in Brain Science 2010*, pp. 62–70, Dana Press, New York.

Ginsburg, KR. (2007). The importance of play in promoting healthy child development and maintaining strong parent-child bonds. *Pediatrics*, 119, 1, 182–191.

Gluckman, PD & Hanson, MA. (2004). Living with the past: Evolution, development and patterns of disease. *Science*, 305, 5691, 1733–1736.

Goh, YI & Koren, G. (2008). Folic acid in pregnancy and fetal outcomes. *Journal of Obstetrics and Gynaecology*, 28, 1, 3–13.

Goldberg, E. (2009). *The New Executive Brain: Frontal Lobes in a Complex World*, Oxford University Press, Oxford.

Goldman-Rakic, PS (1992). Working memory and the mind. *Scientific American*, 267, 3, 110–117.

Goldstein, MH & Schwade, JA. (2008). Social feedback to infants' babbling facilitates rapid phonological learning. *Psychological Science*, 19, 5, 515–523.

Goleman, D. (1995). *Emotional Intelligence: Why it Can Matter More Than IQ*, Bantam Books, New York.

Goleman, D. (2006). *Social Intelligence: The New Science of Human Relationships*, Random House, London.

Gopnik, A. (2009). *The Philosophical Baby: What Children's Minds Tell Us About Truth, Love, and the Meaning of Life*, Picador, New York.

Gopnik, A, Meltzoff, AN & Kuhl, PK. (1999). *The Scientist in the Crib: What Early Learning Tells Us About the Mind*, HarperCollins Publishers Inc, New York.

Goswami, U. (2004). Annual review: Neuroscience and education. *British Journal of Educational Psychology*, 74, 1, 1–14.

Greenough, WT, Black, JE & Wallace, CS. (1987). Experience and brain development. *Child Development*, 58, 3, 539–559.

Greenough, WT & Black, JE. (1992). Induction of brain structure by experience: Substrates for cognitive development. In MR Gunnar & CA Nelson (eds.), *Developmental Behavioral Neuroscience: The Minnesota Symposia on Child Psychology*, vol. 24, pp. 155–200, Lawrence Erlbaum and Associates, Mahwah, New Jersey.

Grille, R. (2005). *Parenting for a Peaceful World*, Longueville Media, Alexandria, NSW.

Grossman, AW, Churchill, JD, McKinney, BC, Kodish, IM, Otte, SL & Greenough, WT. (2003). Experience effects on brain development: Possible contributions to psychopathology. *Journal of Child Psychology and Psychiatry*, 44, 1, 33–63.

Gunnar, MR. (1998). Quality of early care and buffering of neuroendocrine stress reactions: Potential effects on the developing human brain. *Preventive Medicine: An International Journal Devoted to Practice and Theory*, 27(2), 208-211.

Gunnar, MR. (2001). Effects of early deprivation: Findings from orphanage-reared infants and children. In CA Nelson & M Luciana (eds.), *Handbook of Cognitive Neuroscience*, pp. 617–629, MIT Press, Cambridge, Massachusetts.

Gunnar, MR, & Davis, EP. (2003). Stress and emotion in early childhood. In RM Lerner & MA Easterbrooks (eds.), *Handbook of Psychology, Vol. 6. Developmental Psychology*, pp. 113–134, Wiley & Sons Inc, New York.

Gur, RC, Turetsky, BI, Matsui, M, Yan, M, Bilker, W, Hughett, P and Gur, RE. (1999). Sex differences in brain gray matter and white matter in healthy young adults: Correlations with cognitive performance. *The Journal of Neuroscience*, 19, 10, 4065–4072.

Gurian, M. (2001). *Boys and Girls Learn Differently*, Jossey-Bass, San Francisco.

Gurian, M & Stevens, K. (2005). *The Minds of Boys: Saving Our Sons From Falling Behind in School and Life*, Jossey-Bass, San Francisco.

Halpern, DF. (2009). *Sex Differences in Cognitive Abilities*, 3rd edn, Lawrence Erlbaum Associates Inc, New Jersey.

Hamann, S. (2005). Sex differences in the responses of the human amygdala. *The Neuroscientist*, 11, 4, 288–293.

Hannaford, C. (2005). *Smart Moves: Why Learning is Not All in Your Head*, 2nd edn, Great River Books, Alexander, Salt Lake City.

Hardiman, MM. (2003). *Connecting brain research with effective teaching: The brain-targeted teaching model*, Scarecrow Press Inc, Lanham, Maryland.

Hardiman, MM & Denckla, MB. (2010). The science of education: Informing teaching and learning through the brain sciences. In D Gordan (ed.), *Cerebrum: Emerging Ideas in Brain Science 2010*, pp. 3–11, Dana Press, New York.

Harris, JR. (2009). *The Nurture Assumption: Why Children Turn Out the Way They Do*. Free Press, New York.

Healy, J. (1998). *Failure to Connect: How Computers Affect Our Children's Minds—For Better and Worse*, Simon and Schuster, New York.

Healy, J. (2004). *Your Child's Growing Mind: Brain Development and Learning From Birth to Adolescence*, Broadway Books, New York.

Hebb, DO. (1949). *The Organization of Behavior: A Neuropsychological Theory*, John Wiley & Sons, New York.

Hensch, TK. (2005). Critical period mechanisms in developing visual cortex. *Current Topics in Developmental Biology*, 69, 215–237.

Herschkowitz, N & Herschkowitz, EC. (2004). *A Good Start in Life: Understanding Your Child's Brain and Behaviour from Birth to Age 6*, (2nd edn). Dana Press, New York.

Hertzman, C. (1999). The biological embedding of early experience and its effects on health in adulthood. *Annals of the New York Academy of Sciences*, 896, 1, 85–95.

Hillman, CH, Castelli, DM, Buck, SM. (2005). Aerobic fitness and neurocognitive function in healthy preadolescent children. *Medicine and Science in Sports and Exercise*, 37, 11, 1967–1974.

Hillman, CH, Erickson, KI & Kramer, AF. (2008). Be smart, exercise your heart: Exercise effects on brain and cognition. *Nature Reviews Neuroscience*, 9, 1, 58–65.

Hillman, CH, Buck, SM, Themanson, JR, Pontifex, MB, Castelli, DM. (2009). Aerobic fitness and cognitive development: Event-related brain potential and task performance indices of executive control in preadolescent children. *Developmental Psychology*, 45, 1, 114–129.

Hines, M. (2004). *Brain Gender*, Oxford University Press, New York.

Hirsch-Pasek, K & Golinkoff, RM, Eyer D. (2004). *Einstein Never Used Flashcards: How Our Children Really Learn — And Why They Need to Play More and Memorize Less*, Rodale, New York.

Holowka, S & Pettito, LA. (2002). Left hemisphere cerebral specialization for babies while babbling. *Science*, 297, 5586, 1515.

Hooper, J & Teresi, D. (1986). *The Three-pound Universe: Revolutionary Discoveries About the Brain — From Chemistry of the Mind to the New Frontiers of the Soul*, G.P. Putnam's Sons, New York.

Horvath-Dallaire, D & Weinraub, M. (2005). Predicting children's separation anxiety at age 6: The contributions of infant–mother attachment security, maternal sensitivity, and maternal separation anxiety. *Attachment and Human Development*, 7, 4, 398–408.

Howard, PJ. (2006). *The Owner's Manual for the Brain: Everyday Applications from Mind-Brain Research*, 3rd edn, Bard Press, Austin.

Howe, ML & Courage, ML. (2004). Demystifying the beginnings of memory. *Developmental Review*, 24, 1, 1–5.

Hubel, DH & Wiesel, TN. (1970). The period of susceptibility to the physiological effects of unilateral eye closure in kittens. *The Journal of Physiology*, 206, 419–436.

Huesmann, LR. (2007). The impact of electronic media violence: Scientific theory and research. *Journal of Adolescent Health*, 41, 6, S6–S13.

Huttenlocher, PR. (2002). *Neural Plasticity: The Effects of Environment on the Development of the Cerebral Cortex*, Harvard University Press, Cambridge, Massachusetts.

Immordino-Yang, MH & Damasio, A. (2007). We feel, therefore we learn: The relevance of affective and social neuroscience to education. *Mind, Brain and Education*, 1, 1, 3–10.

Izard, CE. (2007). Basic emotions, natural kinds, emotion schemas, and a new paradigm. *Perspectives on Psychological Science*, 2, 3, 260–280.

James, W. (2007). *The Principles of Psychology: Volume 1*, Cosimo Books Inc, New York. (Original work published in 1890).

Jensen, E. (2006). *Enriching the Brain: How to Maximize Every Learner's Potential*, Jossey-Bass, San Francisco.

Johnson, DE. (2001). The impact of orphanage rearing on growth and development. In CA Nelson (ed.), *The Effects of Adversity on Neurobehavioral Development: Minnesota Symposia on Child Psychology*, pp. 113–162, Lawrence Erlbaum Associates Inc, Mahwah, New Jersey.

Johnson, MH. (2001). Functional brain development in humans. *Nature Reviews: Neuroscience*, 2, 7, 475–483.

Jorg, T, Davis, B & Nickmans, G. (2007). Towards a new, complexity science of learning and education. *Educational Research Review*, 2, 2, 145–156.

Kagan, J & Herschkowitz, N. (2005). *A Young Mind in a Growing Brain*, Lawrence Erlbaum Associates Inc, Mahwah, New Jersey.

Kahn, CA, Kelly, PC & Walker, WO. (1995). Lead screening in children with attention deficit hyperactivity disorder and developmental delay. *Clinical Pediatrics*, 34, 9, 498–501.

Kandel, ER. (2001). The molecular biology of memory storage: A dialogue between genes and synapses. *Science*, 294, 5544, 1030–1038.

Kandel, ER. (2009). The biology of memory: A forty-year perspective. *The Journal of Neuroscience*, 29, 41, 12,748–12,756.

Kandel, ER, Schwartz, JH & Jessell, TM. (2000). *Principles of Neural Science*, 4th edn, McGraw-Hill, New York.

Karmarkar, UR & Dan, Y. (2006). Experience-dependent plasticity in adult visual cortex. *Neuron*, 52, 4, 577–585.

Kerr, JFR, Wyllie, AH & Currie, AR. (1972). Apoptosis: A basic biological phenomenon with wide-ranging implications in tissue kinetics. *British Journal of Cancer*, 26, 4, 239–257.

Keuroghlian, AS & Knudsen, EI. (2007). Adaptive auditory plasticity in developing and adult animals. *Progress in Neurobiology*, 82, 3, 109–121.

Kimura, D. (1999). *Sex and Cognition*, MIT Press, Cambridge, Massachusetts.

Kimura, D. (2004). Human sex differences in cognition: Fact, not predicament. *Sexualities, Evolution and Gender*, 6, 1, 45–53.

King, S & Laplante, DP. (2005). The effects of prenatal maternal stress on children's cognitive development: Project Ice Storm. *Stress*, 8, 1, 35–45.

Knight, GP, Guthrie, IK, Page, MC & Fabes, RA. (2002). Emotional arousal and gender differences in aggression: A meta-analysis. *Aggressive Behavior*, 28, 5, 366–393.

Kochanska, G. (2001). Emotional development in children with different attachment histories: The first three years. *Child Development*, 72, 2, 474–490.

Kochanska, G, Coy, KC & Murray, KT. (2001). The development of self-regulation in the first four years of life. *Child Development*, 72, 4, 1091–1111.

Kolb, B. (2009). Brain and behavioural plasticity in the developing brain: Neuroscience and public policy. *Paediatrics & Child Health*, 14, 10, 651–652.

Kosfeld, M, Heinrichs, M, Zak, PJ, Fischbacher, U, & Fehr, E. (2005). Oxytocin increases trust in humans. *Nature*, 435, 7042, 673–676.

Kotulak, R. (1997). *Inside the Brain: Revolutionary Discoveries of How the Mind Works*, Andrews McMeel Publishing, Kansas City.

Knudsen, EI. (2004). Sensitive periods in the development of the brain and behavior. *Journal of Cognitive Neuroscience*, 16, 8, 1412–1425.

Kramer, MS, Aboud, F, Mironova, E, Vanilovich, I, Platt, RW, Matush, L, Igumnov, S, Fombonne, E, Bogdanovich, N, Ducruet, T, Collet, JP, Chalmers, B, Hodnett, E, Davidovsky, S, MD, Skugarevsky, O, Trofimovich, O, Kozlova, L & Shapiro, S. (2008). Breastfeeding and child cognitive development: New evidence from a large randomized trial. *Archives of General Psychiatry*, 65, 5, 578–584.

Krause, K, Bochner, S, Duchesne, S, & McMaugh, A. (2010). *Educational Psychology for Learning and Teaching*, 3rd edn, Thomson Learning Australia, Melbourne.

Krcmar, M. (2010). Assessing the research on media, cognitive development and infants: Can infants really learn from television and videos? *Journal of Children and Media*, 4, 2, 119–134.

Kuhl, PK, Tsao, F-M, & Liu, H-M. (2003). Foreign-language experience in infancy: Effects of short-term exposure and social interaction on phonetic learning. *Proceedings of the National Academy of Sciences, USA*, 100, 15, 9096–9101.

Kuhl, PK, Stevens, E, Hayashi, A, Deguchi, T, Kiritani, S & Iverson, P. (2006). Infants show a facilitation effect for native language phonetic perception between 6 and 12 months. *Developmental Science*, 9, 2, F13–F21.

Kuhl, PK. (2004). Early language acquisition: Cracking the speech code. *Nature Reviews Neuroscience*, 5, 11, 831–843.

Kuhl, PK. (2007). Is speech learning 'gated' by the social brain?. *Developmental Science*, 10, 1, 110–120.

Kuhl, PK. (2010). Brain mechanisms in early language acquisition. *Neuron*, 67, 5, 713–727.

Lafreniere, P. (2009). A functionalist perspective on social anxiety and avoidant personality disorder. *Development and Psychopathology*, 21, 4, 1065–1082.

Lagattuta, KH, & Wellman, HM. (2002). Differences in early parent–child conversations about negative versus positive emotions: Implications for the development of psychological understanding. *Developmental Psychology*, 38, 4, 564–580.

Lamb, ME, Teti, DM, Bornstein, MH & Nash, A. (2002). Infancy. In M Lewis (ed.), *Child and Adolescent Development: A Comprehensive Textbook*, 3rd edn, pp. 293–324, Lippincott Williams & Wilkens, Philadelphia.

Laplante, DP, Barr, RG, Brunet, A, Galbaud Du Fort, G, Meaney, ML, Saucier, J, Zelazo, PR & King, S. (2004). Stress during pregnancy affects general intellectual and language functioning in human toddlers. *Pediatirc Research*, 56, 3, 400–410.

Lazarus, RS. (1999). *Stress and Emotion: A Synthesis*, Springer Publishing Company Inc, New York.

Lecanuet, JP, Fifer, WP, Krasnegor, NA & Smotherman, WP (eds). (1995). *Fetal Development: A Psychobiological Perspective*, Lawrence Erlbaum Associates, Publishers, Hillsdale, New Jersey.

LeDoux, J. (1998) *The Emotional Brain: The Mysterious Underpinnings of Emotional Life*, Simon & Schuster Inc, New York.

LeDoux, J. (2000). Emotion circuits in the brain. *Annual Review of Neuroscience*, 23, 155–184.

LeDoux, J. (2002). *The Synaptic Self: How Our Brains Become Who We Are*, Penguin Books, New York.

Lee, HJ, Macbeth AH, Pagani JH & Young, WS. (2009). Oxytocin: The great facilitator of life. *Progress in Neurobiology*, 88, 2, 127–151.

Legato, M. (2002). *Eve's Rib: The Groundbreaking Guide to Women's Health*, Three Rivers Press, New York.

Legato, MJ. (2005). *Why Men Never Remember and Women Never Forget*, Rodale, New York.

Lenroot, RK & Giedd, JN. (2007). The structural development of the human brain as measured longitudinally with magnetic resonance imaging. In D Coch, KW Fisher & G Dawson (eds.), *Human Behaviour, Learning and the Developing Brain: Typical Development*, pp. 50–73, The Guildford Press, New York.

Lesch, KP & Merschdorf, U. (2000). Impulsivity, aggression, and serotonin: A molecular psychobiological perspective. *Behavioral Sciences and the Law*, 18, 5, 581–604.

Levitt, P. (2003). Structural and functional maturation of the developing primate brain. *The Journal of Pediatrics*, 143, 4, 35–45.

Lewis, MH, Gluck, JP, Beauchamp, AJ, Keresztury, MF & Mailman, RB. (1990). Long-term effects of early social isolation in *Macaca mulatta*: Changes in dopamine receptor function following apomorphine challenge. *Brain Research*, 513, 1, 67–73.

Littlefield-Cook, J & Cook, G. (2009). *Child Development: Principles and Perspectives*, 2nd edn, Pearson, Boston.

Linebarger, DL & Walker, D. (2005). Infants' and Toddlers' Television Viewing and Language Outcomes. *American Behavioral Scientist*, 48, 5, 624–645.

Lozoff, B. (2000). Perinatal iron deficiency and the developing brain. *Pediatric Research*, 48, 2, 137–139.

Lupien, SJ, Maheu, F, Tu, M, Fiocco, A & Schramek, TE. (2007). The effects of stress and stress hormones on human cognition: Implications for the field of brain and cognition. *Brain and Cognition*, 65, 3, 209–237.

Lutchmaya, S, Baron-Cohen, S & Raggatt, P. (2001). Foetal testosterone and vocabulary size in 18- and 24-month-old infants. *Infant Behavior and Development*, 24, 4, 418–424.

Lynn, R. (1993). Nutrition, IQ and physical stature. In PA Vernon (ed.), *Biological Approaches to the Study of Human Intelligence*, pp. 243–258, Abblex, Norwood, New Jersey.

Majdan, M & Shatz, CJ. (2006). Effects of visual experience on activity-dependent gene regulation in cortex. *Nature Neuroscience*, 9, 5, 650–665.

Mares, S, Newman, L & Warren, B. (2005). *Clinical Skills in Infant Mental Health: The First Three Years*, 2nd edn, ACER Press, Camberwell, Victoria.

Martin, LJ, Spicer, DM, Lewis, MH, Gluck, JP & Cook, LC. (1991). Social deprivation of infant rhesus monkeys alters the chemoarchitecture of the brain: Subcortical Regions. *The Journal of Neuroscience*, 11, 11, 3344–3358.

MacLean, PD. (1990). *The Triune Brain in Evolution: Role in Paleocerebral Functions*, Plenum Publishing, New York.

McClelland, MM, Cameron, CE, Connor, CL, Farris, CL, Jewkes, AM & Morrison, FJ. (2007). Links between behavioral regulation and preschoolers' literacy, vocabulary, and math skills. *Developmental Psychology*, 43, 4, 947–959.

McDevitt, TM & Ormrod, JE. (2007). *Child Development and Education*, 3rd edn, Pearson Education Inc, Upper Saddle River, New Jersey.

McEwen, BS. (2002). *The End of Stress as We Know It*, John Henry Press, Washington DC.

McEwen, BS & Norton Lasley, E. (2005). The end of sex as we know it. *Cerebrum*, 7, 4, 1–15.

McEwen, BS. (2006). Protective and damaging effects of stress mediators: Central role of the brain. *Dialogues in Clinical Neuroscience*, 8, 4, 367–381.

McGaugh, JL. (2004). The amygdala modulates the consolidation of memories of emotionally arousing experiences. *Annual Review of Neuroscience*, 27, 1–28.

Meaney, MJ. (2010). Epigenetics and the biological definition of gene and environment interactions. *Child Development*, 81, 1, 41–79.

Medina, J. (2010). *Brain Rules for Baby: How to Raise a Smart and Happy Child from Zero to Five*, Pear Press, Seattle, Washington.

Mehler, J, Jusczyk, P, Lambertz, G, Halsted, N, Bertoncini, J & Amiel-Tison, C. (1988). A precursor of language acquisition in young infants. *Cognition*, 29, 2, 143–178.

Meyer-Bahlburg, HFL, Dolezal, C, Baker, SW, Carlson, AD, Obeid, JS, & New, MI. (2004). Prenatal androgenization affects gender-related behavior but not gender identity in 5–12-year-old girls with congenital adrenal hyperplasia. *Archives of Sexual Behavior*, 33, 2, 97–104.

Miller, DF. (2007). *Positive Child Guidance*, 5th edn, Thomson Delmar Learning, New York.

Milunsky, A, Jick, H, Jick, SS, Bruell, CL, MacLaughlin, DS, Rothman, KJ, & Willett, W. (1989). Multivitamin/folic acid supplementation in early pregnancy reduces the prevalence of neural tube defects. *Journal of the American Medical Association*, 262, 20, 2847–2852.

Moir, A & Jessel, D. (1998). *Brainsex: The Real Difference Between Men and Women*, Arrow Books, London.

Mulder, EJH, Robles de Medina, PG, Huizink, AC, Van den Bergh, BRH, Buitelaar, JK & Visser, GHA. (2002). Prenatal maternal stress: Effects on pregnancy and the (unborn) child. *Early Human Development*, 70, 1 & 2, 3–14.

Mulinare, J, Cordero, JF, Erickson, JD & Berry, RJ. (1988). Periconceptional use of multivitamins and the occurrence of neural tube defects. *Journal of the American Medical Association*, 260, 21, 3141–3145.

Munkata, Y. (2004). Computational cognitive neuroscience of early memory development. *Developmental Review*, 24, 1, 133–153.

Nagel, MC. (2006). *Boys Stir Us: Working with the Hidden Nature of Boys*, Hawker-Brownlow Education, Melbourne.

Nagel, MC. (2008). *It's a Girl Thing*, Hawker-Brownlow Education, Melbourne.

Nagel, MC. (2009). Mind the mind: Understanding the links between stress, emotional well-being and learning in educational contexts. *The International Journal of Learning*, 16, 2, 33–42.

Nagel, MC. (2011). Student learning. In Churchill, R, Ferguson , P, Godinho, S, Johnson, N, Keddie, A, Letts, W, McGill, M, MacKay, J, Moss, J, Nagel, M, Nicholson, P & Vick, M, *Teaching — Making a Difference*, pp. 68–105, John Wiley & Sons Australia, Milton, Queensland.

Nagy, E, Loveland, KA, Kopp, M, Orvos, H, Pal, A & Molnar, P. (2001). Different emergence of fear expressions in infant boys and girls. *Infant Behavior and Development*, 24, 2, 189–194.

National Scientific Council on the Developing Child. (2004). *Young Children Develop in an Environment of Relationships*, Working Paper No. 1, retrieved 10 October 2010 from http://developingchild.harvard.edu/index.php/resources/reports_and_working_papers/working_papers/wp1/

National Scientific Council on the Developing Child. (2005). *Excessive Stress Disrupts the Architecture of the Developing Brain*, Working Paper No. 3, retrieved 10 October 2010 from http://developingchild.harvard.edu/index.php/library/reports_and_working_papers/working_papers/wp3/

National Scientific Council of the Developing Child. (2007). *The Science of Early Childhood Development: Closing the Gap Between What We Know and What We Do*, retrieved 10 October 2010 from http://developingchild.harvard.edu/library/reports_and_working_papers/science_of_early_childhood_development/

Neisser, U. (2004). Memory development: New questions and old. *Developmental Review*, 24, 1, 154–158.

Nelson, CA. (1999). Neural plasticity and human development. *Current Directions in Psychological Science*, 8, 2, 42–45.

Nelson, CA. (2000). Neural plasticity and human development: The role of early experience in sculpting memory systems. *Developmental Science*, 3, 2, 115–136.

Nelson, CA, de Haan, M, and Thomas, KM. (2006). *Neuroscience and Cognitive Development: The Role of Experience and the Developing Brain*, John Wiley & Sons Inc, New York.

Newton, M. (2004). *Savage Girls and Wild Boys: A History of Feral Children*, Picador, New York.

Nobile, M, Giorda, R, Marino, M, Carlet, O, Pastore, V, Vanzin, L, Bellina, M, Molteni, M, Battaglia, M. (2007). Socioeconomic status mediates the genetic contribution of the dopamine receptor D4 and serotonin transporter linked promoter region repeat polymorphisms to externalization in preadolescence. *Development and Psychopathology*, 19, 4, 1147–1160.

Owen, AM, Hampshire, A, Grahn, JA, Stenton, R, Dajani, S, Burns, AS, Howard, RJ, and Ballard, CG. (2010). Putting brain training to the test. *Nature*, 465, 7299. 775–778.

Panksepp, J. (2004). *Affective Neuroscience: The Foundations of Human and Animal Emotions*, Oxford University Press, New York.

Panksepp, J. (2007). Can PLAY diminish ADHD and facilitate the construction of the social brain? *Journal of the Canadian Academy of Child and Adolescent Psychiatry*, 16, 2, 57–66.

Pasterski, VL, Geffner, ME, Brain, C, Hindmarsh, P, Brook, C & Hines, M. (2005). Prenatal hormones and postnatal socialization by parents as determinants of male-typical toy play in girls with congenital adrenal hyperplasia. *Child Development*, 76, 1, 264–278.

Pellegrini, AD, Dupuis, D & Smith, PK. (2007). Play in evolution and development. *Developmental Review*, 27, 2, 261–276.

Pinker, S. (2009). *How the Mind Works*, WW Norton & Company Inc, New York.

Plotnik, R & Kouyoumdjian, H. (2010). *Introduction to Psychology*, 9th edn, Wadsworth Publishing Company, Belmont, California.

Pollak, SD. (2003). Experience-dependant affective learning and risk for psychopathology in children. *Annals of the New York Academy of Sciences*, 1008, 102–111.

Pollak, SD, Nelson, CA, Schlaak, MF, Roeber, BJ, Wewerka, SS, Wiik, KL, Frenn, KA, Loman, MM & Gunnar, MR. (2010). Neurodevelopmental effects of early deprivation in postinstitutionalized children. *Child Development*, 81, 1, 224–236.

Pontifex, MB, Raine, LB, Johnson, CR, Chaddock, L, Voss, MW, Cohen, NJ, Kramer, AF, & Hillman, CH. (2011). Cardiorespiratory fitness and the flexible modulation of cognitive control in preadolescent children. *Journal of Cognitive Neuroscience*, 23, 6, 1332–1345.

Posner, MI & Rothbart, MK. (2000). Developing mechanisms of self-regulation. *Development and Psychopathology*, 12, 3, 427–441.

Posner, MI & Rothbart, MK. (2007). *Educating the Human Brain*, The American Psychological Association, Washington.

Power, C & Hertzman, C. (1997). Social and biological pathways linking early life and adult disease. *British Medical Bulletin*, 53, 1, 210–221.

Purves, D, Augustine, GJ, Fitzpatrick, D, Hall, WC, LaMantia, AS, McNamara, JO & White, LE (eds.). (2008). *Neuroscience*, 4th edn, Sinauer Associates Inc, Sunderland, Massachusetts.

Rakic, P. (1990). Principles of neural cell migration. *Experientia*, 46, 9, 882–891.

Rakic, P. (2002). Genesis of neocortex in human and nonhuman primates. In M Lewis (ed.) *Child and Adolescent Psychiatry: A Comprehensive Textbook*, 3rd edn, Lippincott, Williams & Wilkins, Philadelphia, Pennsylvania.

Ramey, C & Ramey, S. (1999). *Right From Birth: Building Your Child's Foundation for Life — Birth to 18 Months*, Goddard Press Inc, New York.

Ratey, JJ. (2001). *A User's Guide to the Brain: Perception, Attention and the Four Theaters of the Brain*, Vintage Books, New York.

Ratey, JJ. (2008). *Spark: The Revolutionary New Science of Exercise and the Brain*, Little, Brown and Company, New York.

Raver, CC. (2002). Emotions matter: Making the case for the role of young children's emotional development for early school readiness. *Social Policy Report*, 16, 3, 3–18.

Reis, HT, Sheldon, KM, Gable, SL, Roscoe, J & Ryan, RM. (2000). Daily well-being: The role of autonomy, competence, and relatedness. *Personality and Social Psychology Bulletin*, 26, 4, 419–435.

Renner, MJ & Rosenzweig, MR. (1987). *Enriched and Impoverished Environments: Effects on Brain and Behavior*, Springer, New York.

Restak, R. (2001). *Mozart's Brain and the Fighter Pilot: Unleashing Your Brain's Potential*, Three Rivers Press, New York.

Rimm-Kaufman, SE, Early, DM, Cox, MJ, Saluja, G, Pianta, RC, Bradley, RH & Payne, C. (2002). Early behavioral attributes and teachers' sensitivity as predictors of competent behavior in the kindergarten classroom. *Journal of Applied Developmental Psychology*, 23, 4, 451–470.

Robinson, K. (2001). *Out of Our Minds: Learning To Be Creative*, Capstone Publishing, West Sussex.

Roberts, JE, & Bell, MA. (2002). The effects of age and sex on mental rotation performance, verbal performance, and brain electrical activity. *Developmental Psychobiology*, 40, 4, 391–407.

Ropper, A & Samuels, M. (2009). *Adams and Victor's Principles of Neurology*, 9th edn, McGraw Hill, New York.

Rosenzweig, MR, Krech, D, Bennett, EL & Diamond, MC. (1962). Effects of environmental complexity and training on brain chemistry and anatomy: A replication and extension. *Journal of Comparative and Physiological Psychololgy*, 55, 4, 429–437.

Rothbart, MK & Bates, JE. (2006). Temperment. In W Damon, RM Lerner & N Eisenberg (eds.), *Handbook of Child Psychology, Volume 3: Social, Emotional, and Personality Development*, 6th edn, pp. 99–166, John Wiley & Sons Inc, Hoboken, New Jersey.

Roth-Hananiaa, R, Davidov, M & Zahn-Waxler, C. (2011). Empathy development from 8 to 16 months: Early signs of concern for others. *Infant Behavior & Development*, 34, 3, 447–458.

Ruble, DN & Martin, CL & Berenbaum, SA. (2006). Gender development. In N Eisenberg (ed.), *Handbook of Child Psychology Volume 3: Social, Emotional, and Personality Development*, pp. 858–932, Wiley & Sons Inc, New York.

Rueda MR, Fan, J, McCandliss, BD, Halparin JD, Gruber DB, Lercari LP, & Posner, MI. (2004). Development of attentional networks in childhood. *Neuropsychologia*, 42, 8, 1029–1040.

Rutter, M, Moffitt, TE, & Caspi, A. (2006). Gene–environment interplay and psychopathology: Multiple varieties but real effects. *Journal of Child Psychology and Psychiatry*, 47, 3 & 4, 226–261.

Sai, FZ. (2005). The role of the mother's voice in developing mother's face preference: Evidence for intermodal perception at birth. *Infant and Child Development*, 14, 1, 29–50.

Salovey, P & Grewal, D. (2005). The science of emotional intelligence. *Current Directions in Psychological Science*, 14, 6, 281–285.

Savage-Rumbaugh S & Lewin, R. (1994). *Kanzi: The Ape at the Brink of the Human Mind*, John Wiley & Sons, New York.

Sax, L. (2005). *Why Gender Matters: What Parents and Teachers Need to Know about the Emerging Science of Sex Differences*, Doubleday, New York.

Scarr, S & Weinberg, FA. (1983). The Minnesota adoption studies: Genetic differences and malleability. *Child Development*, 54, 2, 260–267.

Schoenthaler, SJ & Bier, ID. (2000). The effect of vitamin-mineral supplementation on juvenile delinquency among American schoolchildren: A randomized, double-blind placebo-controlled trial. *The Journal of Alternative and Complementary Medicine*, 6, 1, 7–17.

Scheonthaler, SJ & Bier, ID, Young, K, Nichols, D & Jansenns, S. (2000). The effect of vitamin-mineral supplementation on the intelligence of American schoolchildren: A randomized, double-blind placebo-controlled trial. *The Journal of Alternative and Complementary Medicine*, 6, 1, 19–29.

Schmidt, LA, & Fox, NA. (2002). Molecular genetics of temperamental differences in children. In J Benjamin, RP Ebstein, & RH Belmaker (eds.), *Molecular Genetics and the Human Personality*, pp. 247–257, American Psychiatric Publishing Inc, Washington.

Schuengel, C, Oosterman, M & Sterkenburg, PS. (2009). Children with disrupted attachment histories: Interventions and psychophysiological indices of effects. *Child and Adolescent Psychiatry and Mental Health*, 3, 26, 1–10.

Seltzer, LJ, Ziegler, TE & Pollak, SD. (2010). Social vocalizations can release oxytocin in humans. *Proceedings of the Royal Society, B — Biological Sciences,* 277, 1694, 2661–2666.

Seltzera, LJ, Prososkia, AR, Zieglerc, TE & Pollak, SD. (2012). Instant messages vs. speech: Hormones and why we still need to hear each other. *Evolution and Human Behavior,* 33, 1, 42–45.

Selye, H. (1974). *Stress Without Distress,* Lippincott Williams & Wilkins, Philadelphia.

Selye, H. (1975). Confusion and controversy in the stress field. *Journal of Human Stress,* 1, 2, 37–44.

Selye, H. (1975). Stress and distress. *Comprehensive Therapy,* 1, 8, 9–13.

Shaffer, DR & Kipp, K. (2010). *Developmental Psychology: Childhood and Adolescence,* 8th edn, Wadsworth, Belmont, California.

Shaw, GM, Schaffer, D, Velie, EM, Morland, K & Harris JA. (1995). Periconceptional vitamin use, dietary folate, and the occurrence of neural tube defects. *Epidemiology,* **6, 3, 219–226.**

Shaywitz, BA, Shaywltz, SE, Pugh, KR, Constable, RT, Skudlarski, P, Fulbright, RK, Bronen, RA, Fletcher, JM, Shankweiler, DP, Katz, L & Gore, JC. (1995). Sex differences in the functional organization of the brain for language. *Nature,* 373 6515, 607–609.

Shonkoff, JP & Phillips, DA (eds.). (2000). *From Neurons to Neighborhoods: The Science of Early Childhood Development,* National Academy Press, Washington.

Shonkoff, JP, Boyce, WT & McEwen, BS. (2009). Neuroscience, molecular biology and the childhood roots of health disparities: Building a new framework for health promotion and disease prevention. *Journal of the American Medical Association,* 301, 21, 2252–2259.

Shonkoff, JP. (2010). Building a new biodevelopmental framework to guide the future of early childhood policy. *Child Development,* 81, 1, 357–367.

Shonkoff, JP and Levitt P. (2010). Neuroscience and the future of early childhood policy: Moving from why to what and how. *Neuron,* 67, 5, 689–691.

Shore, R. (1997). *Rethinking the Brain: New Insights into Early Development,* Families and Work Institute, New York.

Sibley, BA & Etnier, JL. (2003). The relationship between physical activity and cognition in children: A meta-analysis. *Pediatric Exercise Science,* 15, 3, 243–256.

Siegel, DJ & Nurcombe, B. (2002). Development of attention, perception and memory. In M Lewis (ed.), *Child and Adolescent Development: A Comprehensive Textbook* (3rd edn), pp. 227–238, Lippincott Williams & Wilkens, Philadelphia.

Siegel, DJ. (2011). *Mindsight: The New Science of Personal Transformation,* Bantam Books, New York.

Sisk, CL & Foster, DL. (2004). The neural basis of puberty and adolescence. *Nature Neuroscience,* 7, 10, 1040–1047.

Slykerman, RF, Thompson, JMD, Becroft, DMO, Robinson, E, Pryor, JE, Clark, PM, Wild, CJ & Mitchell, EA. (2005). Breastfeeding and intelligence of preschool children. *Acta Paediatrica*, 94, 7, 832–837.

Smith, PF, Darlington, CL & Zheng, Y. (2010). Move it or lose it: Is stimulation of the vestibular system necessary for normal spatial memory? *Hippocampus*, 20, 1, 36–43.

Sousa, D. (2005). *How the Brain Learns to Read*, Corwin Press, Thousand Oaks, California.

Sousa, D. (2006). *How the Brain Learns*, 3rd edn, Corwin Press, Thousand Oaks, California.

Sowell, ER, Peterson, BS, Thompson, PM, Welcome, SE, Henkenius, AL & Toga, AW. (2003). Mapping cortical change across the human lifespan. *Nature Neuroscience*, 6, 3, 309–315.

Spearman, C. (1904). 'General intelligence' objectively determined and measured. *American Journal of Psychology*, 15, 2, 201–293.

Sprenger, M. (2008). *The Developing Brain: Birth to Age Eight*, Corwin Press, Thousand Oaks, California.

Sroufe, LA, Egeland, B & Kreutzer, T. (1990). The fate of early experience following developmental change: Longitudinal approaches to individual adaptation in childhood. *Child Development*, 61, 5, 1363–1373.

Sroufe, LA, Carlson, EA, Levy, AK & Egeland, B. (1999). Implications of attachment theory for developmental psychopathology. *Development and Psychopathology*, 11, 1, 1–13.

Stamm, J. (2008). *Bright From the Start: The Simple Science-Backed Way to Nurture Your Child's Developing Mind From Birth to Age 3*, Gotham Books, New York.

Strauch, B. (2003). *The Primal Teen: What the New Discoveries About the Teenage Brain Tell Us About Our Kids'*, Doubleday, New York.

Sunderland, M. (2008). *The Science of Parenting*, DK Publishing, New York.

Swann, AC. (2003). Neuroreceptor mechanisms of aggression and its treatment. *Journal of Clinical Psychiatry*, 64, supp 4, 26–35.

Sylwester, R. (2005). *How to Explain a Brain: An Educator's Handbook of Brain Terms and Cognitive Processes*, Corwin Press, Thousand Oaks, California.

Sylwester, R. (2007). *The Adolescent Brain: Reaching for Autonomy*, Corwin Press, Thousand Oaks, California.

Tamis-LeMonda, CS, Bornstein, M & Baumwell, L. (2001). Maternal responsiveness and children's achievement of language milestones. *Child Development*, 72, 3, 748–767.

Tamis-LeMonda, CS & Bornstein, M. (2002). Maternal responsiveness and early language acquisition. *Advances in Child Development and Behavior*, 29, 89–127.

Tamis-LeMonda, CS, Shannon, JD, Cabrera, NJ & Lamb, ME. (2004). Fathers and mothers at play with their 2- and 3-year-olds: Contributions to language and cognitive development. *Child Development*, 75, 6, 1806–1820.

Taylor, JB. (2008). *My Stroke of Insight: A Brain Scientist's Personal Journey*, Viking Penguin, New York.

Teicher, MH. (2002). Scars that won't heal: The neurobiology of child abuse. *Scientific American*, 286, 3, 68–75.

Teicher, MH, Andersen, SL, Polcari, A, Anderson, CM, Navalta, CP & Kim, DM. (2003). The neurobiological consequences of early stress and childhood maltreatment. *Neuroscience and Biobehavioral Reviews*, 27, 1 & 2, 33–44.

Thomas, A & Chess, S. (1977). *Temperament and Development*, Brunner/Mazel, New York.

Thompson, RA, Meyer, S & McGinley, M. (2005). Understanding values in relationship: The development of conscience. In M Killen & JG Smetana (eds.), *Handbook of Moral Development*, pp. 267–297, Lawrence Erlbaum Associates, Mahwah, New Jersey.

Thompson, RA, & Lagatutta, K. (2008). Feeling and understanding: Early emotional development. In K McCartney & D Phillips (eds.), *The Blackwell Handbook of Early Childhood Development*, pp. 317–337, Blackwell Publishing, Oxford.

Tomporowski, PD, Lambourne, K & Okumura, MS. (2011). Physical activity interventions and children's mental function: An introduction and overview. *Preventive Medicine*, 52, supp 1, S3–S9.

U.S. Department of Health and Human Services, Centers for Disease Control and Prevention. (2010). The Association Between School-Based Physical Activity, Including Physical Education, and Academic Performance. http://www.cdc.gov/healthyyouth/health_and_academics/pdf/pa-

Valiente, C, Lemery-Chalfant, K, Swanson, J & Reiser, M. (2008). Prediction of children's academic competence from their effortful control, relationships and classroom participation. *Journal of Educational Psychology*, 100, 1, 67–77.

Vondra, JI, Shaw, DS, Swearingen, L, Cohen, M & Owens, EB. (2001). Attachment stability and emotional and behavioral regulation from infancy to preschool age. *Development and Psychopathology*, 13, 1, 13–33.

Vouloumanos, A & Werker, JF. (2004). Tuned to the signal: The privileged status of speech for young infants. *Developmental Science*, 7, 3, 270–276.

Wager, TD & Ochsner, KN. (2005). Sex differences in the emotional brain. *NeuroReport*, 16, 2, 85–87.

Wiesel, T. (1982). Postnatal development of the visual cortex and the influence of environment. *Nature*, 299, 583–592.

Wiesel, TN & Hubel, DH. (1963). Single cell response in striate cortex of kittens deprived of vision in one eye. *Journal of Neurophysiology*, 26, 1003–1017.

Willingham, DT. (2009). *Why Don't Students Like School: A Cognitive Scientist Answers Questions About How the Mind Works and What It Means for the Classroom*, Joseey-Bass, San Francisco.

Willingham, DT. (2011). Can teachers increase students' self-control? *American Educator*, 35, 2, 22–27.

Wismer-Fries, AB & Pollak, SD. (2007). Emotion processing and the developing brain. In D Coch, KW Fisher & G Dawson (eds.), *Human Behavior, Learning and the Developing Brain: Typical Development*, pp. 329–362, The Guilford Press, New York.

Wolfe, CD & Bell, MA. (2007). The integration of cognition and emotion during infancy and early childhood: Regulatory processes associated with the development of working memory. *Brain and Cognition*, 65, 1, 3–13.

Wolfe, P. (2001). *Brain Matters: Translating Research into Classroom Practice*, Association for Supervision and Curriculum Development, Alexandria, Virginia.

Wolfe, P & Nevills, P. (2004). *Building the Reading Brain — Pre K–3*. Corwin Press, Thousand Oaks, California.

Yang, C, Huang, C & Hsui, K. (2004). Behavioral stress modifies hippocampal synaptic plasticity through corticosterone-induced sustained extracellular signal-regulated kinase/mitogen-activated protein kinase activation. *The Journal of Neuroscience*, 24, 4, 11,029–11,034.

Zimmerman, FJ, Christakis, DA & Meltzoff, AN. (2007). Associations between media viewing and language development in children under age 2 years. *The Journal of Pediatrics*, 151, 4, 364–368.

Zimmerman, FJ, Gilkerson, J, Richards, JA, Christakis, DA, Xu, D, Gray, S & Yapanel, U. (2009). Teaching by listening: The importance of adult-child conversations to language development. *Pediatrics*, 124, 1, 342–349.

Index